T0294521

The Manual of Strategic Planning for Cultural Organizations

The Manual of Strategic Planning for Cultural Organizations

A Guide for Museums, Performing Arts, Science Centers, Public Gardens, Heritage Sites, Libraries, Archives, and Zoos

Gail Dexter Lord

Kate Markert

ROWMAN & LITTLEFIELD
Lanham • Boulder • New York • London

Published by Rowman & Littlefield
A wholly owned subsidiary of The Rowman & Littlefield Publishing Group, Inc.
4501 Forbes Boulevard, Suite 200, Lanham, Maryland 20706
www.rowman.com

Unit A, Whitacre Mews, 26-34 Stannary Street, London SE11 4AB

British Library Cataloguing in Publication Information Available

Library of Congress Cataloging-in-Publication Data Available

Names: Lord, Gail Dexter, 1946-, author. | Markert, Kate, 1952-, coauthor.
Title: The manual of strategic planning for cultural organizations : a guide for museums, performing arts,
    science centers, public gardens, heritage sites, libraries, archives, and, zoos / Gail Dexter Lord and Kate
    Markert.
Other titles: Manual of strategic planning for museums
Description: Lanham : Rowman & Littlefield, 2017. | Includes bibliographical references and index.
Identifiers: LCCN 2016047499 (print) | LCCN 2017004481 (ebook) | ISBN 9781538101308 (hardcover :
    alkaline paper) | ISBN 9781538101315 (paperback : alkaline paper) | ISBN 9781538101322 (electronic)
Subjects: LCSH: Museums—Planning—Handbooks, manuals, etc. | Museums—Management—
    Handbooks, manuals, etc. | Strategic planning—Handbooks, manuals, etc. | Gardens—Planning—
    Handbooks, manuals, etc. | Zoos—Planning—Handbooks, manuals, etc. | Historic sites—Planning—
    Handbooks, manuals, etc. | Libraries—Planning—Handbooks, manuals, etc. | Performing arts—
    Societies, etc.—Planning—Handbooks, manuals, etc.
Classification: LCC AM121 .L67 2017 (print) | LCC AM121 (ebook) | DDC 069/.068—dc23
LC record available at https://lccn.loc.gov/2016047499

∞™ The paper used in this publication meets the minimum requirements of
American National Standard for Information Sciences—Permanence of Paper for
Printed Library Materials, ANSI/NISO Z39.48-1992.

Printed in the United States of America

Contents

Figures and Tables

Figures

Tables

Preface

Gail Lord

The cultural sector has grown in size and dynamism during the decade since we published *The Manual of Strategic Planning* in 2007. This sector has embraced change, becoming more outward looking; adopting new technologies; transforming governance structures; embracing diversity; and collaborating with artists, scientists, and communities in unexpected ways. The underlying philosophy of both books is that strategic planning presents an organization with the opportunity to determine its optimal future through a process of self-assessment, external engagement, study, and debate. A major difference between the two is that the first was devoted to museums and the current book is for performing arts, libraries, gardens, parks, science centers, festivals, historic sites, and museums—from A (art) to Z (zoos).

There are compelling reasons for our expanded focus. Today we work in an environment that places a high priority on creativity and innovation, which is the point of convergence for all cultural organizations. We live in a world that is becoming more urban and dense, which creates a need for the public realm that cultural institutions provide. Cultural workers balance the imperatives of sustainability, community health, individual wellness, migration, inequality, and education with the demands of professionalism in art and science. It was thus a welcome challenge for us to formulate a strategic planning process for these new realities.

Strategic planning is the joint responsibility of the governing body and staff leadership, and it is one of the few aspects of nonprofit cultural management shared by the board and staff. This manual is for board members familiar with corporate boards but new to the cultural sector, where boards measure success against mission and social benefit rather than profit. It is for staff leaders who strive for excellence and seek a planning process that will align their entire organization with agreed goals. It is for students, artists, scientists, government officials, funders, community leaders, volunteers, and cultural participants who want to understand the functions of cultural organizations and why strategic planning improves performance, leading to measurable impact and soft power.

We begin the journey in chapter 1 with *why*, introducing the forces of change that motivate strategic plans and the central role of mission and vision statements to the functions and governance of a range of cultural organizations. Chapter 2 recommends *when* to conduct your strategic plan. Chapter 3 describes *who* is involved in strategic planning and *what* the ten key steps in the planning process are. Chapter 4 explains *how* to engage with your constituencies to create a meaningful and relevant plan. In chapter 5 we explore how to cultivate strategic thinking throughout your organization, and chapter 6 tells you everything you need to know for a successful strategic planning retreat. Chapter 7 details how to write the plan, while chapter 8 focuses on how best to implement it. "Measuring what matters" is the theme of chapter 9, which contains practical suggestions on incorporating evaluation into the plan and its implementation. You may want to read chapter 10 first because it presents frequently asked questions about strategic planning and candid answers about what can go wrong and how to fix it.

We hope you will find this book a helpful guide as you contemplate and conduct your strategic plan, and that you will be as inspired as we are by the case study examples throughout. The journey from contemplating the plan to implementing it is challenging, surprising, and even enjoyable. On the way, participants may ask "Are we there yet?" This manual will help you answer that and other questions on every step of the exciting journey to create the optimal future for your cultural organization.

Acknowledgments

This book is indebted to the board and staff leaders of cultural organizations around the world with whom I have worked on strategic plans in my capacity as copresident of Lord Cultural Resources. Among the many distinguished participants in that process of practice and debate, I am especially grateful to Kate Markert, my coauthor and collaborator on so many projects. Since the first edition of this manual in 2007, we have perfected the art of completing each other's sentences wherever we are.

Thanks are due to all those who contributed case studies to this volume and to John Hoal, who reviewed some of the manuscript. Your collective commitment to innovation through strategic planning for gardens, performing arts, collecting institutions, libraries, and science centers will inspire readers as you have inspired Kate and me.

I am grateful to my colleagues at Lord Cultural Resources who have worked with me to develop the strategic planning process. Special thanks to Michelle Selmen and Loren Aytona for assembling the manuscript and creating the tables and figures; to Rebecca Frerotte, who prepared the bibliography and glossary, conducted research, and proofread; and to Mira Ovanin, my executive assistant, who managed the correspondence, the editorial process, and (most challenging of all) me.

As always, our publishers, Rowman & Littlefield, have been splendidly supportive. I am particularly grateful to Charles Harmon who encouraged Kate and me to expand our successful first edition about museums into the uncharted territory of the not-for-profit cultural sector. Production editor Kellie Hagan was patience personified.

Finally, my most profound thanks to my husband and partner Barry Lord, my inspiration personally and professionally in this book as in everything.

Gail Lord

★ ★ ★

First, I'd like to thank my colleague and friend Gail Lord for inviting me to be her coauthor for the update of our original strategic planning book. We have worked together on plans for Hillwood Estate, Museum & Gardens; the Walters Art Museum; and the Cleveland Museum of Art, and we have spoken together on a number of professional panels in the United States and Europe. It has been a great pleasure to work with Gail in all the situations we have tackled together.

Thanks also to the board members at Hillwood Estate, Museum & Gardens for their support of my work on the book and to my colleagues there for sharing their expertise and specific sections of Hillwood's plan for inclusion here. The Cleveland board and staff participated in what remains an exemplary strategic planning process with the late director Robert P. Bergman, whose brilliance and good humor will always be remembered.

Finally, my deepest appreciation to my husband Bunky, who relinquished a summer to allow me time to devote to this book.

Kate Markert

Chapter 1

Why Conduct a Strategic Plan?

Few announcements in the life of a cultural organization can inspire more varied responses than "It's time for a new strategic plan."

The board and staff who want to see major changes will welcome strategic planning. Others will insist that strategic planning is a waste of time. There will be a group who feel that strategic planning has nothing to do with them. And some people will recoil in fear because a new strategic plan means staff and board reorganization or changes to programs and projects.

Everyone is right, in part. There are no guarantees that the outcomes of a strategic planning process will be entirely successful or that all change will be positive for everyone. Strategic planning is as much art as science. However, if the process is well planned, open, and transparent, the result is more likely to be a relevant, inspiring, and effective plan that brings the board, staff, and stakeholders together around common goals that will move your cultural organization forward and improve its performance.

Cultural institutions generally conduct strategic plans for any or all of the following reasons:

- To improve performance.

- To qualify for funding because government, foundation, and private donors increasingly require evidence of a current strategic plan.

- To achieve accreditation from a recognized authority.

- To prepare the groundwork for a major expansion or new initiatives.

- To motivate staff and board.

- To replace or update the previous strategic plan that has run its course.

- To address the forces of change in the environment, both internal and external.

Whatever the main motivation for conducting a strategic plan, the benefits can be enormous because strategic planning is the best tool for determining your direction and course of action for the next three to five years.

Forces of Change

Ours is a time of massive global change: new technologies, growing urbanization, the transformation of societies from production-based to knowledge-based economies, and a major shift in energy sources from carbon-based sources to renewables, to name but a few. Increasingly, cultural organizations of all types are making change and helping people creatively adapt to change. Here are a few of the ways that cultural organizations are responding:

- Libraries make digital technology accessible to all.

- Science centers model new forms of creativity.

- Theaters transform lives through storytelling.

- Festivals build civil society.

- Museums mediate cultural change.

- Historic sites explore the diversity of the past.

- Parks and gardens advocate for environmental sustainability, public health, and wellness.

- Zoos save species.

While many cultural professionals like to pronounce that "we can't be all things to all people," cultural organizations have, in fact, become many more things to many more people than we ever dreamed. Strategic planning is an important tool for determining which functions your cultural organization should focus on and how you should do so.

Furthermore, there can no longer be a discrete list of cultural organization types because twenty-first-century change also blurs boundaries. Libraries and parks display exhibitions. Museums host performance art. Gardens preserve specimens. And most cultural entities participate in spectacles and festivals. This explosion of new roles and functions has been stimulated by forces not only within the sector but also in society. By way of example, here are eighteen external and internal factors that are driving change.[1]

External Factors

1. The number of cultural organizations in many areas has more than doubled, providing greater public access but also increasing competition for scarce leisure time.

2. The dramatic increase in educational attainment has resulted in higher rates of cultural participation.

3. New government and foundation policies link funding to the fulfillment of educational and social objectives.

4. Cultural tourism is a growth industry highly reliant on museums, gardens, and festivals.

5. Security threats, energy price fluctuations, and other unforeseen changes can produce sudden negative effects on attendance and increase costs such as insurance.

6. Government funding has steadily declined.

7. Cities, where the majority of cultural organizations are located, have risen as centers of economic power.

8. Soft power, or influence through peaceful means, is most effective when exercised through independent nonprofit cultural organizations.[2]

9. Electronic and digital technologies are accessible through the Internet.

10. Public demand for big events, from "blockbuster" exhibitions and shows to immersive experiences, has increased.

Internal Factors

1. The increasing professionalism of cultural organization staff leads to new ideas, higher performance standards, and bigger salaries.

2. Staff demonstrate enthusiasm for improving visitor services.

3. More board members from the corporate sector expect that nonprofit culture should operate "like businesses."

4. Operating costs are rising.

5. A growing need exists to store collections, archives, stories, and knowledge for all cultural types.

6. The number of cultural buildings with impressive architecture has increased.

7. More administrative personnel are needed to increase revenue streams.

8. National and global cultural systems and "brands" are developing.

Much of the change in cultural organizations—such as a focus on visitors rather than connoisseurship—has been in response to these and other forces. The resultant stresses have made it increasingly difficult to recruit directors, balance budgets, and forge cohesive organizations.

The usual tensions between research and showmanship or between tradition and the avant-garde have never been greater. The rapid growth of specializations such as fundraising, marketing, sponsorship, retail, food services, product development, licensing, and space rental have tipped the balance of staff numbers away from creative, curatorial, scientific, and conservation functions toward administration. Education departments, although of growing importance in theaters, gardens, and zoos, are still marginal to the axis of power in fundraising potential and spectacle. And many trustees and directors—frustrated with what they perceive as the slow pace of internal change—often turn to architects for a solution. A new or expanded building is frequently seen as the fast track to reinvention and adaptation.

It may seem obvious that building a new extension cannot resolve the crises of change. However, the excitement generated by a design and construction process can go a very long way toward *stimulating* institutional change. For libraries that have reinvented themselves as places of information rather than repositories for books, new buildings and branches have been key to meeting changing public needs and announcing their new roles.

Of course, many of these external and internal pressures do create a demand for more space—for the storage and care of growing collections, for new and larger galleries, for experimental performance spaces, or for more revenue generation capability. But even when this is true, there are likely to be additional deep-rooted issues that can be resolved only by a strategic planning process.

Strategic planning is the opportunity the cultural organization has to assess its situation, discuss the options, and determine a course of action—that is, *to be the real architect of its own future.*

Strategic planning is the process of determining the optimal future for an organization and the changes required to achieve the future.

Organizations that engage in a thorough and transparent strategic planning process can expect the following outcomes:

- A shared vision of the future among the board and staff

- A common understanding of the mission

- Agreement on major goals for the next three to five years and how to achieve them

- Consensus on how to measure the achievement of those goals

Conducting and writing a strategic plan takes from six months to one year. The timeline for implementing a strategic plan is about three to five years.

Understanding Your Cultural Organization

To appreciate the benefits of working together as an entire organization and taking the time and the risk to conduct a strategic plan, it is useful to review the basic characteristics of nonprofit cultural organizations to which this book is dedicated. The overview of four categories of cultural organizations provided below highlights some of the issues you may encounter and demonstrates key similarities among organizations, such as the need for teamwork among departments, the constancy of change, and public service.

Collection-Related Organizations: Museums, Zoos, Historic Sites, Botanical Gardens, and Science Centers

Collecting institutions are uniquely concerned with collecting, preserving, and displaying material cultural heritage and communicating its meaning—whether it arises from works of art, archaeological and historical artifacts, natural history specimens, living species, or scientific knowledge.

Some new museum types focus more on communication than collections, such as children's museums, which specialize in communicating material heritage to children; science centers, which specialize in communicating scientific concepts; and "idea museums," which collect stories and explore ideas like peace in the Musée pour la Paix in France or human rights in the Canadian Museum For Human Rights. However, insofar as the material heritage of the subject is at their core, these have been accepted as museums, and they attest to the flexibility of the museum as a medium.

These two aspects of museums—collecting or preserving, and communicating—are inextricably linked and differentiate museums from other cultural institutions, but they also create a tension. Gifted directors and inspired senior management teams can orchestrate this tension as a creative force.

When strategically planning for museums and other collecting institutions, it is essential to revisit the question of balance between these two polarities. Should we invest more in our collections in the next five years, or is it time to focus on renewing our displays? Obtaining the agreement of the entire staff and the board on this question is the only way to ensure that the decision will be carried out at the highest level of quality and creativity.

Collecting institutions fulfill fifteen to twenty functions that can be organized around collections/curatorial, communication/programming, and administration/management.

Collections/Curatorial

The main functions that pertain to the collections and curatorial arena include the following:

- research

- acquisition

- documentation

- conservation

- collection management

- exhibition

Communications/Programming

Communication and programming work includes a number of functions:

- interpretation

- education

- activities

- visitor services

- marketing

- publication

Administration/Management

Management facilitates the progressive interaction between the collections-focused and communications-focused functions toward the achievement of agreed-upon goals that move the museum, zoo, or historic site forward. As part of this process, administration must attend to several areas:

- buildings and grounds

- security, health, and safety

- human resources

- finances

- board management

- external and government relations

- earned-income streams (food services, shops, facility rentals, admissions)

- long-range planning

- fundraising and development

As with so much contemporary thought and organization, boundaries among these broad functional areas are blurred. Because the various functions are interrelated, teamwork is a valuable tool. But the differences in outlook and training between a highly skilled conservator and a highly skilled marketer make teamwork a challenge. Strategic planning can bring staff together to construct common goals and objectives—and to work together to implement the plan. Marketing and conservation can work together to promote the little-known contributions the museum or zoo, for example, is making to scientific and art historical research.

Each of the fifteen to twenty functions is guided by a policy that establishes its qualitative parameters. The appropriate senior manager prepares the policies for the director, who then recommends them for board approval. Collections policies, for instance, are quite complex, defining the type, condition, and provenance of what can be collected and how the items or species are to be accessioned and preserved. Similarly, exhibition policies indicate the philosophy of research and communication underpinning the exhibitions, the procedure for making decisions on the changing exhibition program, and the roles and responsibilities of staff departments, the director, the board, and sponsors.

The senior management team of all cultural organizations—which usually consists of the director and the deputy directors of each main area (collections, communications/programs, and administration)—guides the institution in several ways (also illustrated in figure 1.1):

- inspiring the staff and the board toward fulfilling the museum's mission and vision

- communicating the museum's mandate both internally and externally

- evaluating the efficiency and effectiveness of all museum functions

- leading the institution toward its goals

- controlling the attainment of tasks and objectives by staff and volunteers

Performing Arts

Performing arts disciplines include theater, dance, music, opera, cirque, and spoken word, to name a few. Within these categories, performing arts organizations may specialize in different genres and time periods, such as:

- Shakespearean theater

- classical jazz

- contemporary playwrights

- Middle Eastern dance

- Cantonese shadow puppetry

- baroque music on period instruments

Performing arts organizations generally are either presenting or producing institutions. Presenting organizations present productions created by other organizations; they provide the venue and

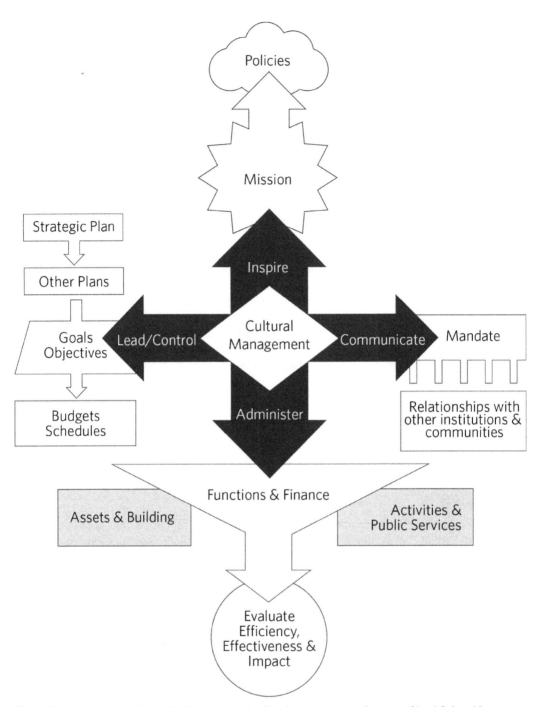

Figure 1.1 Strategic planning in the big picture of cultural management. *Courtesy of Lord Cultural Resources.*

sometimes lead marketing efforts. For instance, Lincoln Center for the Performing Arts in New York presents acts such as the classical Chinese dance and music company Shen Yun. However, like some other presenting institutions, they also originate some programming, such as the Lincoln Center Festival and Midsummer Night Swing.

Producing organizations fund and create original or revival works. They are responsible for production activities such as casting, set, lighting, design, costumes, and everything else required to put on a show. Producing organizations may not have the venues required to present their shows. They rent rehearsal space until the production goes into preview at a presenting house. Fiasco Theater, for example, is an ensemble theater company that produces classic and new plays—the company has been in residence at many universities across the United States.

Most performing arts institutions can be organized around two overarching functions: artistic and administrative. As a result, many performing arts organizations have two equal directors: artistic director and managing director, each of whom has several spheres of responsibility.

Artistic

- literary management

- programming

- casting

- education

- production (stage, set, audio, lighting, costume)

Administrative

- operations (human resources, buildings and grounds, security, event rentals)

- ticketing

- marketing, branding, and partnerships

- finance

- external and government relations

- fundraising or development

- education

Challenges

All cultural organizations and their departments face pressure resulting from constrained resources that can lead to "turf wars," siloed departments, lack of coordination, and aging infrastructure. In response, there is always a strong push to bring in more money and satisfy donors' requests.

The development department is positioned to balance the best interests of donors with the artistic mission and vision of the performing arts organization. As a result of this situation, challenges often arise in servicing the request of a donor; such challenges may manifest themselves in interactions between the development department and the programming and marketing departments. For example, a donor may want a certain show produced next season or specific placement on the organization's website and brochures. Strategic planning can uncover these conflicts and create goals and objectives to streamline communication and remedy potential issues.

Public Service Role

Not-for-profit cultural organizations operate to fulfill a mission, usually one that contributes to society as a public service.

Educational programming can affect communities through performances, education, training, and career development opportunities for both children and adult learners. Educational programs are attractive to potential funders. Performing arts organizations also provide a public service through accessibility. Often, the cost of admission is seen as the only barrier to access, but accessibility is equally, if not more related to the relevance of the content for the audience, particularly underserved groups within a community. The Albany Park Theater Project in Chicago creates powerful theater with youth from diverse backgrounds as writers and performers.

Libraries

Libraries provide access to information that has been recorded.

Access to information is the defining characteristic of libraries because the medium on which the information has been recorded has changed over the long history of libraries, from stone tablets to scrolls and books and now to digital and electronic multimedia forms. More than any other cultural institution, libraries have been transformed by the digital shift and must constantly adapt to rapid technological development. Libraries use strategic planning to challenge assumptions and to execute new directions so that they are prepared for whatever new information media comes next.

The primary role of librarians is to assist people in effectively and efficiently retrieving and accessing information. Users drive the nature of the information the library collects and the programming and services the library offers.

There are four main categories of libraries:

- academic libraries serving colleges and universities

- public libraries serving local communities

- school libraries serving school-age groups from kindergarten to grade 12

- special libraries, including specialized fields such as art, medical, and law

Libraries in all categories have three basic functions: public services, technical services, and management. Each of those functions, in turn, includes several areas of responsibility.

Public Services

- circulation

- reference, which includes directional questions, information retrieval, ready or quick reference, and in-depth research

- outreach services

- programming

- library promotion and marketing

- advocacy

Technical Services

- collection development, which includes both digital and physical collections

- acquisitions

- cataloguing

- processing

Management/Administration

- buildings and grounds

- security, health, and safety

- human resources

- finances

- board management

Why Conduct a Strategic Plan?

- external and government relations

- earned-income streams (food services, shops, facility rentals, admissions)

- long-range planning

- fundraising and development

In smaller libraries, librarians may provide both public and technical services, whereas in larger institutions these areas of work are often separate with many specialist departments in each. Staff members must understand the ways their roles are interrelated and support one another. Administration and management should foster relationships among departments and specialists.

Library management differs from most cultural institutions in that libraries are mainly situated as line departments or agencies within larger organizations: the academic library in the university, the public library to the library board, with an arm's-length relationship with their municipal government, and the special library within a corporate setting. These owning or governing organizations add complexity to library management. Library directors will be accountable to several entities: their own board, the larger department within which they report, and government. Many museums, zoos, science centers, and performing arts centers are also owned and operated by government either as line departments or as arm's-length agencies, but the majority are independent not-for-profits with independent governing boards, and this model tends to be dominant even in city, state, and federal institutions. In order to encourage more private funding for these cultural organizations, foundations are established. Many municipal libraries and museums are government funded and operated but have independent foundations.

Therefore, when formulating organizational goals and objectives, library leadership must also consider the institutional context and ensure that their vision, mission, and goals closely align with the mandates of parent and governing institutions.

Gardens and Parks

Gardens preserve and display plants for the enjoyment and education of the public; they also conduct research and develop cultivation methods to improve the lives of plants.

There are many different types of gardens: Botanical gardens, which are collecting institutions, collect plants, preserve plant records, undertake scientific research on plants in their collections, and display and communicate this information to other gardens, scientific institutions, and the public. Horticultural gardens collect and cultivate plants for their beauty and the pleasure they bring, focusing on display and on cultivation to improve species. Arboreta are devoted to the cultivation and preservation of different species of trees or shrubs for study and display. And historic gardens are cultural landscapes of a specific historic period, often attached to historic buildings and sites. There are also therapeutic or healing gardens, remembrance gardens, art gardens, and sculpture parks.

Public parks are public spaces with trees, flower beds, lawns, and paths.

A destination public park has cultural significance due to a particular combination of location, role in the community, size, history, landscaping, or embedded attractions that draw a diversity of users and uses.

Gardens and parks reflect the changing realities of the environment and the communities and visitors they serve. As a result, the functions of gardens and parks have expanded to include a greater responsibility for environmental stewardship and additional functions as cultural and educational organizations. Gardens and parks are today a platform for multisensory discovery, learning, and entertainment. To support and maximize these new functions, the management of gardens and parks has become more strategic, data driven, and collaborative.

Gardens and parks fulfill a multitude of functions grouped into three main categories with specialist staff in each:

Horticulture and Science

- collections

- identification

- display and design

- conservation

- science and research

Public Services

- education

- activities and events

- public health and wellness

- community formation

- social and economic impact

- performing arts

- interpretation

- exhibition

- marketing

- design and production

- publication

- guest services and earned-income streams (food services, shops, facility rentals, admissions, commercial enterprise)

Administration/Management

- facilities and horticultural support

- security, health, and safety

- human resources

- IT operations and information services

- finances

- external and partner relations

- fundraising

Finding the right balance among these three functions requires a culture of teamwork and innovation. For example, maximizing attendance while preserving species can be a challenge. Some gardens and many parks are in the independent nonprofit sector; many others are owned and operated by government. There is a growing trend for not-for-profit organizations called "conservancies" to raise money to support the educational and horticultural activities of public parks in areas where government cannot fully meet growing demands. Conservancies differ from "friends organizations" because they also participate in park management. Strategic planning is a tool for gardens to plan growth in the context of competing priorities and complex governance.

The Significance of Foundations Statements

Not-for-profit cultural organizations are defined by their foundation statements, which are usually incorporated into their legal framework, whether a legislative act, as is the case for many museums and libraries that are agencies or departments of government, or a constitution and bylaws, as is the case for the many cultural organizations in the charitable or not-for-profit sector.

For-profit cultural organizations such as commercial theaters and attractions focus on differentiating their offerings from competitors through branding. Not-for-profit cultural organizations make use of branding in their marketing strategies as well, but foundation statements guide the entire operation at a high level, sometimes with the force of law. Nonprofits provide their services for less than the cost of producing them.[3] This gap is filled by grants and donations from government, charitable foundations, and individuals; nonprofit organizations are highly accountable for that funding through public scrutiny and tax regulations that allow most such donations to be free of taxes. Foundation statements are important tools for reducing redundancy and duplication of effort and expenses. They also help to ensure that organizations receiving public funds and nontaxed private funds use them for the purposes for which they are intended.

Foundation statements encompass mission, vision, and mandate. By way of example, this section provides definitions of the foundation statements and demonstrates how the statements might evolve in response to external change and leadership in a library system, a science center, and a performing arts center.

The mission states the intent or purpose of the cultural organization, its raison d'être.

For the ABC Library System: To assist our entire community in gaining efficient and effective access to information when they need it and wherever they need it.

For the XYZ Science and Technology Center: To inspire our community with the achievements of science and to stimulate fresh scientific inquiry.

The LMN Performing Arts Center delights our community by hosting performances by innovative and diverse artists from both near and far.

The vision expresses the impact the cultural organization would like to have.

The ABC Library System aspires to expand literacy and the love of reading in our diverse community by sharing all forms of media.

The XYZ Science and Technology Center vision is to create a new generation of scientists.

The LMN Performing Arts Center will inspire future generations to feel, and participate in, the freedom of artistic expression.

The mandate outlines both the range of cultural activities for which the organization takes responsibility (such as types of media, disciplines, and geographic and chronological range) and the organization's reach in terms of audience (whether local, national, or international; focused on a particular age, on families, on seniors, and so on).

The ABC Library System responds to the information needs of all county residents and facilitates communication among them by providing meeting spaces and educational programs.

The XYZ Science and Technology Center focuses on the physical sciences, complementing the Natural History Museum, which concentrates on the biological sciences, of which it has great collections of specimens.

The LMN Performing Arts Center fulfills its mission by hosting local, national, and international performances and by ensuring accessibility to programs on-site and off-site through outreach to community schools and underserved neighborhoods.

The foundation statements of your organization may be all jumbled up in some legislation, in letters patent, or in some minutes of a long-ago board meeting. Wherever they are, you need to find them and unravel the history of the statements. They may have been rewritten for different occasions and now should be analyzed as part of the strategic planning process. Since strategic plans are created or renewed every three to five years, it would be a mistake to think that the foundation statements should be changed each time. However, foundation statements need to be updated when there is reason to do so.

For example, the ABC chief librarian sees a need to revise the current mission statement, which refers only to print materials, to include digital information and multimedia. One of the goals of her or his strategic plan is to acquire digital collections and increase computer capacity.

Meanwhile, the director of the XYZ Science and Technology Center has decided that the Natural History Museum down the road has systematically excluded recent discoveries in genetic science from its research and exhibits of the biological sciences. With the help of some local funders, she wants to expand the center's exhibits to incorporate biological sciences. This does not conflict with the XYZ Science and Technology Center's original mission "to inspire our community with the achievements of science," but it requires a change to the center's mandate, either to include biological sciences or to refer to the applied sciences rather than referencing particular scientific disciplines. Indeed, this could be a matter of discussion with the Natural History Museum. Successful mandates are those that are negotiated rather than proclaimed.

The artistic director of the LMN Performing Arts Center envisions adding a black box theater to the center to accommodate a resident company. This does not conflict with the mission or vision, but it requires an amendment to the mandate, which identifies the center as only presenting performances by outside groups. This change of mandate, if agreed to by the board, would entail many additional changes to be addressed in the strategic plan.

> Strategic planning provides the framework within which the foundation statements can be objectively reviewed and updated.

Notes

1. These factors and others will figure in the environmental scan discussed in chapter 3.

2. "Soft Power is a concept that emerged a quarter century ago to describe international relations based not on military nor economic might but on influence. Soft Power is the ability to influence behavior using persuasion, attraction or agenda setting." Gail Dexter Lord and Ngaire Blankenberg, *Cities Museums and Soft Power* (Washington, DC: Rowman & Littlefield, 2015), 9.

3. "[A museum] typically provides its service to the public without charge or at a price below the cost of producing those services." Stephen Weil, *Making Museums Matter* (Washington, DC: Smithsonian Books, 2002), 38.

Case Study 1.1

The Guggenheim Museum Bilbao Strategic Vision 2020

Juan Ignacio Vidarte

I had the privilege of contributing a case study entitled "Meeting Twenty-First-Century Challenges at the Museo Guggenheim Bilbao" to the *The Manual of Strategic Planning for Museums* (2007); I have now updated it to reflect our strategic planning so far.

Ten years after its opening in 1997, the Guggenheim Museum Bilbao, having achieved the objectives of its previous strategic plans, started a new planning process as a mature institution that aimed to keep its position as a leading museum both in Spain and worldwide. Aware of the need to define its position within an increasingly complex cultural, social, economic, political, and technological context, the museum approached planning in two complementary ways: through the short-term strategic plan for 2009 to 2012 and through the long-term Vision 2020 development. The Vision 2020 was formulated in the following way:

> The Guggenheim Museum Bilbao will be recognized as a European leader in innovation and in the creation of a visitor-centered museum experience. It will play an ever more active role in the Solomon R. Guggenheim Foundation, both in the development of new projects and in specialized training in museum management for the benefit of the Guggenheim Constellation and the creative economy of the Basque Country.

The Vision 2020 should be read in conjunction with the museum's mission statement:

> To collect, preserve, and research modern and contemporary art, and to present it from multiple perspectives within the context of the History of Art, addressing a broad, diverse audience, so as to contribute to the knowledge and enjoyment of art and the values that it represents, within a unique architectural landmark, as an essential part of the Guggenheim network, and a symbol of the vitality of the Basque Country.

The museum upholds certain values that make up its corporate philosophy, the spirit with which the mission is pursued:

> *Sensitivity and respect for art.* We work with artistic sensitivity, and respect for the work of art governs our actions.

> *Integration with the art community.* We contribute to the enrichment of artistic and cultural activity in the Basque Country within the framework of the cultural strategies of its institutions.

> *Commitment to quality.* The success of the Museum involves managerial excellence; this demands quality work.

> *Customer orientation.* Satisfied customers are our only guarantee of a successful future. Thus our priority is to gear our work towards satisfying our clients in all their diversity.

> *Educational orientation.* Facilitating the public's acquaintance with culture and especially with modern and contemporary art is our prime commitment.

Economic orientation. Resource management is optimized in our work to ensure the highest possible degree of self-financing for the Museum.

Integration and cooperation with the Guggenheim Museums. We foster and promote individual and organizational integration with the objectives, culture, and identity of the Solomon R. Guggenheim Foundation.

Commitment to society. The Museum seeks to serve as a symbol of the vitality of the Basque Country and to promote ethical conduct through art.

Confidence in our staff. We encourage participative work based on honesty, trust, integrity, and responsibility, and foster the values of liberty and respect for the individual.

A family-friendly organization committed to respecting diversity and equal opportunity. The Guggenheim Museum Bilbao makes every effort to act in an ethical, socially responsible manner and to promote respect for diversity and equal opportunity, with the goal of facilitating a healthy work-life balance for employees from a gender-conscious perspective.

Since adopting Vision 2020, the Guggenheim Museum Bilbao has embarked on three subsequent strategic plans (for 2009–2012, 2013–2014, and 2015–2017), each including a number of strategic initiatives to achieve its Vision 2020.

In the strategic plan for 2009 to 2012, the Guggenheim Museum Bilbao sought to expand through the innovative concept of "discontinuous" extension, which would not only increase the exhibition space but also combine art, nature, and landscape beauty in a nonurban environment. The museum also reinforced existing relationships with some of the most prestigious contemporary artists. This planned expansion would promote the museum's position as a global and local leader. The main aspirations of this project were to develop new modes of interpretation, to create synergies with the knowledge economy, and to generate wealth, independent resources, and new opportunities for collaboration in the creative society of the Basque Country.

The principal challenge addressed within the 2013–2014 strategic plan was renewing the collaboration agreement with the Solomon R. Guggenheim Foundation. This alliance has undoubtedly generated benefits for the Bilbao Museum, such as the wide recognition of the brand, the quality of the art program, the scope of the relationships with first-rank museum institutions, the economies of scale generated by sharing projects and exhibition tours, the access to the extraordinary Guggenheim Foundation holdings of modern and contemporary art, the implementation of an innovative management model based on private-public participation, and the revenue maximization. In an ever-changing context of increasing competition, renewing the collaboration between the Basque Institutions and the Solomon R. Guggenheim Foundation enabled new projects and formulas to be forwarded within the next ten years. Innovation, creative knowledge, globalization, networking, and identity were considered within the process of continuous improvement and reinvention that presides over the operations of the Guggenheim constellation.

Finally, the strategic initiatives included in the 2015–2017 plan focus on three main lines of work—contents, technology, and stakeholder relations—with the ultimate aim of fulfilling the museum's vision and mission.

Contents

A New Approach to the Art Program

The year 2015 marks the dawn of a new era in the museum's art program, combining exhibitions of the finest quality that appeal to its diverse audiences with a more visible presence of the Guggenheim Collections. In light of the Bilbao Collection's maturity and the fact that many visitors expect to see certain collection pieces when they come, works from the Bilbao holdings will be presented on a more regular basis. In addition, the galleries on the museum's three floors have been assigned different exhibition formats to lend the art program greater stability. The museum continues consolidating its curatorial voice and artistic identity in several ways, most notably by developing in-house projects and coproductions in which Bilbao's curatorial team plays an increasingly important role.

Educational Programs and Didactic Spaces

Innovation, creativity, participation, and experience are some of the pedagogical cornerstones of the Guggenheim Museum Bilbao's current educational program. By taking a holistic approach to education, it offers its target audiences a wealth of knowledge and information about the art program and the building designed by Frank Gehry.

Technology: Digital Information

Changing habits in how people access information and the increasing use of new devices is transforming museums, which are evolving from places of contemplation to hybrid spaces where digital technology is part and parcel of the visitor's experience. As the museum generates content for different formats, there is an opportunity to optimize the transmission of that content using various methods and media. Creating attractive new digital materials and unifying and streamlining those that already exist will improve the visitor experience and meet the needs and expectations of an increasingly diverse audience. The museum will also use digital resources and technology to establish and strengthen relationships with its stakeholders.

Stakeholder Relations

Strengthening Ties with the Community

The museum is aware of the crucial role it has played over the years in changing the public perception and reputation of the city of Bilbao locally, nationally, and internationally. Today, when museums are increasingly expected to be accessible forums of social inclusion, exchange, and dialogue, this strategic initiative aims to strengthen and draw attention to the museum's ties with local individuals and organizations. Putting down stronger "roots" in the community and the local art scene, maintaining programs with an emphasis on social outreach, and creating a network of emotional bonds will allow the museum to identify people with a potential interest in its activities and strengthen ties with them.

Relations with Museum Members

Since its founding, the museum has enjoyed the support of various groups as evident in their visits to the museum and their fidelity and commitment to the institution. One of the strategic initiatives for this period is to strengthen the loyalty of each group by offering benefits tailored to their specific interests, recruiting new supporters into existing groups, and creating new membership and support categories.

Code of Ethics and Best Practices

Best practices, transparency, ethical management, and accountability are hot topics in the governance of public and private institutions today. Therefore, this strategic plan demonstrates the museum's transparent management practices and constant leadership in good governance as a way to connect with society and maintain community trust. A code of ethics and best practices will also highlight the museum's actions and commitments, and the public recognition and distinctions it has earned over the years.

Figure 1.2 Students learn more about Jeff Koons with the Guggenheim Museum Bilbao iTunes U courses. *Courtesy of Erika Ede.*

Case Study 1.2

Why Do You Need Libraries Anyway?
The County of Los Angeles Public Library Strategic Plan

Susan Kent

Challenging the value and future of public libraries has become more common. The rise of the Internet together with increasingly pervasive digital access to the world of information has led people to question the place of public libraries in the community, the need to fund libraries and library facilities, and the role of these public institutions in the future. The public library is certainly changing, with technology revolutionizing the ways in which a public library operates; libraries are morphing from their traditional role as book-centered quiet places to become places for innovation, education, creativity, and learning.

Shifting the goals and objectives of a public institution is not without difficulties and resistance. A public library, a publicly supported entity with a governance structure that includes elected and appointed officials, faces close scrutiny, particularly when financial support is required. With this in mind, every public library in every community must prepare for a future that is subject to rapid and often unexpected change.

The County of Los Angeles Public Library

The County of Los Angeles Public Library in California serves a population of more than 3.3 million people spread over three thousand square miles through eighty-five regional and community libraries, an institutional library, and three bookmobiles. It serves both unincorporated areas of the county as well as forty-nine individual incorporated cities and has to deal with many independent political entities. In 2011, the then library director (now retired) hired a consultant team—MIG of California and S. R. Kent—to work with her and the library staff on a strategic plan that would guide the library's services, collections, and facilities for the next five years. She felt strongly that the development of the plan should also be an opportunity for intensive staff involvement and staff development.

The strategic planning process for the County of Los Angeles Public Library was created to involve as much of the library's service population as possible. A robust public engagement process was developed with many opportunities to learn from the various communities it served. The strategic plan had several purposes:

- to define the role of the library

- to identify needs and desires

- to engage with the future

- to provide staff learning and growth opportunities

- to create and strengthen partnerships and community support

Among the various components of the strategic planning process were the following:

- telephone survey (conducted by Godbe Research)

- stakeholder interviews

- focus groups

- trends report

- expert panel

- staff survey

- online interactive game and survey tool

- scenarios workshop

- staff strategy teams

- electronic magazine version of the strategic plan

Of these, several were noteworthy for their effectiveness in stimulating discussion, new ideas, and excitement.

Expert Panel

Several components of the planning process were targeted at informing key stakeholders, the strategic advisory committee of community leaders, and the staff strategic planning project team about innovative and exciting activities at leading libraries in the United States, similar in size and structure to the County of Los Angeles Public Library. An expert panel of three library leaders from different areas of the United States presented a daylong workshop on libraries as physical space, the public library's role in facilitating early learning and cultivating young readers, techniques used to engage diverse populations, moving from a purely physical space to a digital library with a physical footprint, the impact of e-books and publishing on libraries, the role of librarians now and in the future, and more.

Scenarios Brainstorming Workshop

Based on the information gathered through the stakeholder interviews, strategic advisory committee meetings, the staff strategic planning project team working sessions, the expert panel presentation, and the trends report prepared for this purpose, a discussion of the key challenges and issues facing the library in the next five to ten years was held with the staff strategic planning process team. In addition, the workshop attendees were asked to identify the driving social forces that would affect the library in the years ahead. The staff strategic planning project team spent a day working on four scenarios that addressed four critical issues identified by library staff:

Manual of Strategic Planning for Cultural Organizations

- changes in ownership and licensing library materials

- the role of public space and a redefinition of community

- access to information

- reputation building

The participants looked at the driving forces outside the library that will have the greatest impact on these challenges, as well as the uncertainties that might shape these challenges. Then they created scenarios that addressed these issues. These scenarios formed the basis for the new initiatives adopted later in the process.

Online Game

An online game was developed to gather input from the public regarding library services and priorities. It was available on the library's home page for one month. The game was structured like a film, *Library 2020: The Movie*, and the players created a cartoon-like filmstrip as they answered a variety of questions that included (1) what kinds of things the library should have, (2) what the library should offer on its website, (3) what the library should provide for teens, and (4) how the library can reach out to the community. The online game was intended to be a fun, easy technique to solicit ideas, and almost two thousand participants offered their suggestions.

Trends Report

A trends report was prepared by the consultants to identify trends and questions that the library must consider as it moves forward. The staff strategic planning process team considered these issues as they identified goals and objectives specific to the County of Los Angeles Public Library:

- How can public libraries build a sustainable future in a rapidly evolving technological environment?

- How are collections—paper and electronic—preserved, presented, and disseminated?

- Where is technology taking the library internally and externally?

- What is the library building of the future, and how can libraries be flexible and adaptable as their collections, missions, and uses change over time?

- How can libraries serve new generations of potential library users in buildings and through technology?

- Is there or should there be a new paradigm for public library services?

- What is the role of the library staff in nurturing and supporting innovation and providing training for the public?

- What do the disappearing borders between consuming and creating information mean for library collections and services?

- How does a library negotiate the transition between the passive and active use of library services, including collections, technology, and facilities?

Staff Strategy Teams

After all the presentations, community engagement opportunities, staff participation, and work sessions, eight staff strategy teams were put in place to work on the initiatives for the future. These teams worked together on their own and with the consultants to refine ideas and translate them into achievable goals and objectives. The involvement of library staff throughout the process and, particularly, in developing the final plan language and presentation was impressive. It achieved what the library director hoped for as the process began. Library staff recognized the need for change and innovation. They had real learning opportunities during the process, and many positioned themselves for increasing responsibilities and promotion in the organization. And, most importantly, staff were excited about the library's future because they helped define it.

The County of Los Angeles Public Library Strategic Plan

The County of Los Angeles Public Library updated its mission statement: "The Library gives you freedom to—Explore, Create, Connect—whatever your needs or dreams." This mission, along with its newly articulated values of integrity, customer service, community, invention, collaboration, learning, and sustainability, led directly to the eight initiatives for the future:

- Tell the library's story.

- Affirm the library as a center for learning.

- Expand and support the digital library.

- Transform the role of library as place.

- Support and cultivate the community's creativity.

- Develop the library as a center for community engagement.

- Develop a staff prepared for the future.

- Ensure the financial health of the library.

The County of Los Angeles Public Library's strategic planning process involved many members of its large and diverse community in a multiplicity of ways: surveys, focus groups, stakeholder interviews, an online "game," and a communications plan that used social media and the library's website. Participation of the staff was strongly encouraged and included a staff survey, training staff to conduct focus groups in their local communities, staff project teams, and a major information presentation with questions and answers at the all-staff day. Key community leaders were consulted; for instance, the five members of the county board of supervisors or their representatives were interviewed individually. Every opportunity was given to listen to people, to respond to their ideas and concerns, and to address the question of why the public library is needed. The answer: it is not only needed but also crucial.

Figure 1.3 Libraries are serving a new generation of users through inspiring space and new technology. *Image credit: Open Grid Scheduler / Grid Engine.*

Case Study 1.3

Soft Power and Toronto's Gardiner Museum's Strategic Plan

Kelvin Browne

When I arrived as executive director at the Gardiner Museum in November 2013, I intuited that the future of our museum would be its connection to the community and how it would be of service, how it could open itself to local needs, and how it could communicate the poignant nature of its artifacts rather than just their pedigree. An emotional connection, likely one generated by focusing on the soft notion of clay rather than the hard edge of ceramics, would sustain the museum and lead to its growth. The metaphor is a good one:

clay is malleable, it needs to be shaped to become of use, while the finished object is unchanging and must be accepted on its own terms.

The museum can be a welcoming place once a visitor is through the door. Yet, on the surface, the institution could present something more formidable to the uninitiated—a sleek contemporary building with immaculate displays of extraordinary ceramics, many referencing historic worlds of wealth and splendor, and lectures by world-renowned experts that connoisseurs respect. This "gem of a museum" remains a worthy but remote destination for some.

Of course, we are still celebrating the art of ceramics, which is our mandate. However, this celebration is about the wonder of what people create, the stories they tell through the objects they make, and the beauty these objects add to our lives. Finding ways for the community to need us rather than requiring our audience to become what we need them to be is a challenge all museums must address. How do we make a transition from being an institution driven by the vision of its founders to becoming one that has a vital and audacious brand that represents an authentic experience in an increasingly virtual world? Rather than taking the more traditional approach of institutional power based on prestige and curatorial authority—we know everything and you don't—we believed the way forward was soft power based on shared making, co-creation, and participation. That said, building our curatorial department continues to be essential. The stewardship of our collection remains imperative, but this priority is not readily perceived by the public and hence is not a major factor driving engagement or community support, particularly in terms of revenue.

The Gardiner Museum was a successful institution when I became executive director. It had a superlative permanent collection of ceramics; the collection was not encyclopedic but was a collection of collections of international significance—approximately four thousand objects, including the most important collection of European porcelain and Italian Renaissance maiolica in Canada, as well as ceramics from the ancient Americas, Chinese blue and white porcelain, Japanese porcelain, and contemporary Canadian ceramics. It had a balanced budget for several years and an endowment that provides over a quarter of its approximately $3.5 million annual operating budget. In 2014 we held the thirtieth anniversary celebration of its founding by Toronto businessman George Gardiner, who died in 1997, and his wife, Helen, a driving force at the museum who continued to be very involved until her death in 2008. Many of the museum's most important supporters were their friends.

If soft power was the goal, how did we begin to realize it? My arrival coincided with the initiation of the next three-year strategic planning process; as part of this, we commissioned research about how the museum was perceived and the needs of its stakeholders. The key finding of the research, and the one that substantiated the most compelling comments during the consultation process, was that the museum was doing many of the things it should, but no one knew it, including those most likely to visit or donate. For instance, because the museum's contemporary exhibitions and comprehensive programming were not communicated to a wide audience or packaged in a manner that caught the attention of the media, the museum had an old-fashioned brand—the phrase "dish mausoleum" comes to mind. Even more startling was that many in the public did not know the Gardiner Museum existed at all. For some, even those who lived or worked nearby, it was merely a mysterious building at the top of a flight of stairs, one not intriguing or welcoming enough to visit.

The first issues to be tackled were those of perception—both in terms of the ephemeral, like brand, and the practical, such as signage. You cannot build attendance or donations if few know what you are doing or if those who support you never hear about what their contributions are making happen. Moreover, if the community doesn't feel your museum is engaging them or reflecting their experiences, you will play no role in their lives, however important the collections you steward. Were we talking to ourselves instead of having a dialogue with our community?

Increasing visibility started with a new lighted sign on the plaza and backlit advertising with a bolder, more contemporary design. The plaza signs had an enviable, highly visible perch on a heavily traveled urban arterial road. Creating the signs required increasing the marketing budget, one that had been reduced over the years to sustain high levels of programs and exhibitions that often had low attendance. Efforts to increase awareness of the museum also translated to a greater focus on social media and a major investment in a website that had not been updated for at least eight years. We also reduced the number of major exhibitions and hence were able to invest more in the exhibitions we had, especially in their marketing and installation to enhance the visitor experience.

The museum was in the process of renovating its superb European Porcelain Galleries when I joined. Along the way, the design changed to tell a more visual story, to give the visitor a more immersive experience. One of the outcomes was to recreate an eighteenth-century dessert table in the heart of the gallery. Now people feel they have been invited to a dinner, albeit one held a few centuries ago. The table communicates the collection with the visitor's perspective in mind.

We also wanted to bring the experience of making ceramics closer to the public by adding a clay studio to the lobby. In 2017, visitors will see people or an artist in residence working with clay as they enter. This will enliven the entry experience and provide a sense of the technical mastery of what they are about to see in the galleries. As much as we can, we are putting the heart of the museum out there, almost on the street.

We need community partners to collaborate on programs and help put our museum at the center of their world, at least for a while. It's soft power through collaboration. A good example of this is a show borrowed from the Smithsonian called *Women, Art, and Social Change: The Newcomb Pottery Enterprise*. In addition to ceramics, this exhibition included jewelry, textiles, and bookbinding and was a brilliant snapshot of a time in the late nineteenth and early twentieth centuries when women were given the opportunity to develop a social enterprise when there were few other opportunities for them. It was an excellent historical show and a wonderful exhibition of beautiful objects. However, it was not necessarily relevant to many, especially those not already interested in ceramics or feminist history. This show could become relevant by using it to focus on similar issues today—women in the workplace and the empowerment and freedom that being able to earn a living gives.

The Gardiner Museum collaborated with community-connected partners to achieve this. With Human Rights Watch Canada we presented a lecture on women's rights with an international perspective, with the Next 36 we hosted a panel discussion about women entrepreneurs and the challenges they still face, and we featured products in our shop from the Far and Wide Collective, which helps market products in Canada made by women in developing countries. These and other programs vastly increased the audience for the show. Our collaborators had large networks of supporters, and we were promoted through them. This show demonstrated that we saw ourselves as a catalyst for discussion. This experience clarified the paramount importance of programming for having soft power.

I equate soft power with having influence, being listened to because you have a credible voice, not because you are large. We are not evangelical at the Gardiner, but we are a potent platform for discussing the things our museum cares about. This summer our Community Arts Space program gave five community-based arts groups the use of our main exhibition hall to present their ideas. The request for proposals required that their proposal relate in

Figure 1.4 Visitors, staff, and community partners gathered to celebrate the launch of the Gardiner Museum's new Community Arts Space. Guests were invited to take part in hands-on clay activities and make their mark on the "living sketchbook" that lined the gallery walls. *Courtesy of Jae Yang.*

some way to clay or ceramics, and we received fifty responses! One of the most interesting was a play in which ceramics were made during the performance and the objects were central to the drama. The Community Arts Space is an opportunity for a broad community to work with us and to help us become what we need to be.

Soft power also means being accessible. For example, we became free for visitors eighteen years and younger this year; prior to this, the museum was free to those twelve and under. We are free on Tuesdays for all students. Our new website will also increase accessibility.

We are beginning our next three-year strategic plan soon. Research has shown that perceptions of the museum have changed. Downtown cultural consumers' awareness of us has tripled, and we are beginning to see the benefits of this through sold-out programs, sustained membership levels, and new sources of philanthropic and sponsorship support. Being on the radar is a start, as is the perception that we are a place that is important to the community and where provocative new things can happen. Soft power is opening a new world for our museum.

Chapter 2

When to Conduct a Strategic Plan

Since strategic plans usually apply to a specific time period of three to five years, the main reason for initiating a new plan is that "time is up." Achieving the goals set out in the previous plan provides motivation to undertake a new planning process even sooner. This may mean that your organization should embrace more ambitious goals to take its performance to the next level. There are other reasons to initiate a strategic plan out of sequence, such as the accession of a new director or CEO, a change to the organization's governance, a relocation, the opening of a new branch or building, or a major financial change—from a large bequest to a substantial reduction in sustaining support. Strategic planning is not crisis management; however, if the fundamental governance or financial situation changes, a new or updated strategic plan is needed.

Professional Standards

Increasingly, professional standards across the cultural sector require an up-to-date strategic plan: it may be key to qualifying for government and philanthropic funding and is often a criterion for accreditation, a necessary indicator for support from private and public funders. Accreditation brings other benefits such as exhibition exchange (including animals for zoos), increased status, and attractiveness to top employees. The Association of Zoos and Aquariums advises its members to conduct a strategic master plan to guide development.[1] The Public Library Association offers its members webinars on strategic planning, emphasizing it as "the first step of library growth."[2] The Association of College and Research Libraries advocates for aligning the strategic plans of academic libraries with their broader institutions.[3] In Ontario, Canada, museums wishing to receive government funding (and 91 percent of museums apply) are required to produce and follow short- and long-term plans.[4] The American Public Garden Association's sustainability index is a success measure for gardens that requires a strategic plan to be completed within the following five years.[5] The Commission for Accreditation of Park and Recreation Agencies requires a strategic plan for accreditation.[6] Arts Council England, the Welsh government, Museums Galleries Scotland, and the Northern Ireland Museums Council have standardized accreditation schemes that require strategic plans. Becoming accredited can lead to greater support, in both financial and other forms, from many sources because it demonstrates that the organization has met a professional standard.[7]

The American Alliance of Museums (AAM) is an accrediting body for museum and collecting institutions. Increasingly, U.S. funding authorities are requiring AAM accreditation to qualify for grants. Two core questions guide every AAM accreditation review and assure that the museum is in compliance with national standards:

- How well does the museum achieve its stated mission and goals?

- How well does the museum's performance meet standards and best practices as they are generally understood in the museum field, as appropriate to its circumstances?

The new emphasis on goal attainment and institutional planning is further elaborated in the AAM Accreditation Commission's expectations regarding institutional planning. The commission expects that accreditable museums will have the following characteristics:

- All aspects of the operations are integrated and focused on meeting the institution's mission.

- The governing authority and staff think and act strategically to acquire, develop, and allocate resources to advance the mission of the museum.

- The organization engages in ongoing and reflective institutional planning that involves its audiences and community.

- There are measures of success used to evaluate and adjust the museum's activities.

The emphasis that so many professional associations place not just on the fact of strategic planning but on the quality of the plan shows how accepted it has become as a requirement for well-run institutions and reflects the larger global trend toward careful and considered management and leadership in the nonprofit cultural sector.

New Director

The arrival of a new director often becomes the moment to contemplate a new strategic plan. This is logical, since the new director comes to the organization with a fresh perspective and new ideas. There is a "chicken and egg" question as to whether the strategic plan precedes the director search process or follows the appointment of the new director. The answer is likely both. No one can predict with certainty when a cultural institution will require a new leader. If one is anticipated during the strategic planning process because of, for instance, an impending retirement, then a succession plan should be part of the strategic plan. However, assuming this is not the case, a new or updated strategic plan needs to be in place so that the executive search leads to a good fit between the institution and the prospective candidates. The most successful director searches come out of a process whereby the board has assessed the general direction they envision for the organization and have hired a director with a skill set aligned with that direction. Thus, if the governing group is looking for a change in the new leader, the strategic plan should be updated prior to or as part of the search process. Once the new director is in position, it is advisable to wait a year or two before initiating a new strategic plan to provide time for the director to fully understand the cultural institution, its resources, and its challenges. This "wait time" speaks to the value of having a strategic plan in place prior to the executive search.

New Circumstances

Sometimes circumstances can change dramatically in a short period of time, for better or worse. For example, an institution might receive an enormous windfall from a testamentary gift that provides the opportunity to rethink strategies. Quickly worsening financial circumstances, which many organizations experienced in the years following the global economic crisis of 2008, may also make a serious course correction necessary. In addition, the significant rise in insurance costs can lead to the cancellation of a number of major projects. Skyrocketing fuel prices have increased building occupancy costs, with the result that energy efficiency has become a strategic issue for building operations. Social issues such as the engagement of diversity at the staff, management, and board levels have become more urgent and insistent in many communities. Ethical and legal concerns regarding ownership of collections and relationships between museums and originating communities have assumed critical dimensions for some museums, and the question of cultural appropriation affects all the arts.

Ideally, an institution's staff and board leadership will see opportunities and threats on the horizon and plan for the desired change as part of the annual strategic plan update (see chapter 8).

New and Renewed Facilities and New Location

The need or desire for new facilities can also be the catalyst for a strategic plan. The most logical and efficient sequence of institutional planning begins with a strategic plan that lays out the broad goals and direction for the organization; with that plan as the underpinning, the next step is master planning, where the architecture and programming align with the larger institutional goals. Starting with a new building before strategic goals have been established usually leads to later difficulties when programmatic needs surface that are not supported by the new building spaces (or when new spaces are created for programming that does not take place).

Once the new facility is open and functioning in its new environment, a new or updated strategic plan is required. The Whitney Museum of American Art, whose case study is described below, illustrates the degree of change that its new building and location created for audiences, exhibitions, and management, thus requiring a new strategic plan to realign board, staff, and management.

Readiness Checklist

The following readiness checklist can help you decide when to conduct your strategic plan.

- The director has been at the museum for at least one year.

- The director knows the institution's culture, strengths, and weaknesses.

- The board has confidence in the director's leadership.

- The director and board are committed to the strategic planning process.

- Resources are attainable or at hand to support the planning process.

The strategic planning process requires resources to be carried out effectively. There are grants for strategic planning, but often these grants come under the heading of "building organizational capacity."[8] If your organization has not engaged with strategic planning, money spent to hire skilled planners to help think through the opportunities and issues will be an investment in the institution's future.

On the other hand, if your organization has a culture of planning and skilled staff leadership, it is possible to fine-tune or extend the plan's horizon using in-house resources. In any case, board and staff time needs to be devoted to the process for an effective outcome.

The planning process must be an institutional priority that is given time in the workweek over a number of months. The easiest way to sabotage the planning process is for leadership to assume either that it can happen on top of everything normally done by the various staff members or that hiring an outside planner will eliminate the need for staff to make time for the process during their workdays. The organization can choose not to do a project during the planning time, or it can hire additional staff to give the permanent staff planning time. Board members need to devote time to the process as well. Those who participate on the steering committee will attend extra meetings; there will be additional reading to acquaint everyone with the issues and opportunities; and time will be needed for interviews, discussions, and board workshops.

Time spent planning will result in more efficient alignment across the organization, better communication, and clarity of vision, and this will repay the investment in institutional resources devoted to the process.

Strategic planning provides the entire staff and governing body with an opportunity to set big-picture goals for a foreseeable future of three to five years. The strategic planning process engages all departments in organizing current objectives and tasks, anchored to the actual functions of the organization in a way that also fulfills these broad institutional goals.

An organization can be said to be "in alignment" when all its parts are working toward common goals. This is easy to say but very difficult to do in an organization that is "values-led" rather than "profit-led"—and in an organization comprised of highly creative individuals from many intellectual disciplines.

The next chapter takes on this task of designing a strategic planning process that suits not-for-profit creative organizations, their staffs, and their governing bodies.

Notes

1. Association of Zoos and Aquariums, *The Accreditation Standards and Related Policies, 2016 Edition* (Association of Zoos and Aquariums, 2016), available at www.aza.org/assets/2332/aza-accreditation-standards.pdf.

2. Public Library Association, "It's All in the Planning: Getting Started on Strategic Plans and Development Plans," webinar, February 5, 2014, at www.ala.org/pla/onlinelearning/webinars/ondemand/planning (accessed July 25, 2016).

3. Association of College and Research Libraries, "Assessment in Action: Academic Libraries and Student Success," at www.ala.org/acrl/AiA (accessed July 25, 2016).

4. Ontario Ministry of Tourism and Sport, "Standard for Community Museums in Ontario," last modified November 2, 2015, at www.mtc.gov.on.ca/en/museums/museums_standards.shtml (accessed July 25, 2016).

5. American Public Gardens Association, "Public Garden Sustainability Index: Start Here," at publicgardens.org/sustainability-index/start-here (accessed July 25, 2016).

6. Commission for Accreditation of Park and Recreation Agencies, *National Accreditation Standards*, 5th ed. (National Recreation and Park Association, revised April 2014, amended July 2015), available at www.nrpa.org/uploadedFiles/nrpa.org/Professional_Development/Accreditation/CAPRA/CAPRA-Standards-5th-Edition-2014.pdf.

7. Accredited Museum, *Accreditation Guide, Section One: Organizational Health* (Arts Council England, June 2014), available at www.artscouncil.org.uk/sites/default/files/download-file/FINAL_201406_Guidance-Section1_PrintFriendly.pdf (accessed July 25, 2016).

8. Funding sources that will support building organizational capacity include the Ontario Trillium Foundations "Seed" and "Grow" grants; the Heritage Lottery Fund (HLF) in the United Kingdom, which provides "heritage grants" to hire professional experts to execute their application and projects for truly successful implementation; the Canada Council for the Arts, which provides capacity-building programs including "The Flying Eagle" specifically for aboriginal arts groups; the Alliance for California Traditional Arts' small granting programs that specifically provide project support and capacity building; the Kenneth Rainin Foundation, which launched its capacity-building "Impact Grant" in 2013; and the Ontario Arts Council's Compass grants, which help arts organizations work with outside experts who have specialized knowledge and experience, including strategic and business planning.

Case Study 2.1

It's Time for Strategic Planning at the Whitney Museum of American Art

Amy Roth

A wise museum director recently said, "I've never had so much fun working on a strategic plan." Speaking to our museum's senior staff group, he went on to tell us that, in his long experience working on strategic plans—six plans over five decades in art museums—this was the first one that he has really, truly enjoyed. The reason was simple, he explained: this was the first strategic plan that was not a response to a crisis of leadership, a crisis of finances, or a building project.

Why is this? Why do museums often wait to consider their future aspirations and priorities, with rigor and gravitas, until their circumstances demand it? Why do they delay such critical thinking until their position affords them the least likelihood of dreaming big and then pursuing those dreams?

In my role as chief planning officer of the Whitney Museum of American Art, I am happy to share our experiences of strategic planning on both sides of a major change event—the relocation to a new, significantly larger building in Manhattan's Meatpacking District in May 2015. I share these experiences in order to highlight two moments when an organization should consider strategic planning: (1) following any major change event and (2) when times are good, from a position of strength.

The rationale for strategic planning following a major change event is somewhat obvious, and I will first discuss the Whitney's specific circumstances in highlighting these points. Perhaps more difficult to justify and to execute is strategic planning from a position of strength, absent a major trigger such as a building project. Very fortunately, we have been able to leverage both moments in our current strategic planning process. The first clarified the case and gave us the urgency to get the process going; the second allowed us to capitalize on sound fundamentals to raise the bar even higher—despite having only just recently raised the bar higher than we ever had before.

Not every organization can count on a major, positive change event. It goes without saying that some change events—such as crises of leadership or finances—can be extremely negative and disruptive. Based on our experiences at the Whitney, I hope to make a case for pursuing proactive strategic planning while the going is good—the proverbial making hay while the sun shines—and to suggest a series of critical questions to ask yourself and your organization en route to pulling the strategic planning trigger.

Consistent with our sector's norms, the Whitney's last strategic plan was formulated in anticipation of a "building event." Our new building project gave us a sense of purpose and a tangible, visible milestone against which we could track tactics and activities, recalibrate priorities, and measure successes. With a new building among our end goals, our strategic plan became, very rightly so, the vehicle that (1) connected the museum's mission to our relocation and building project; (2) formally asserted, on paper, the aspirational ideas and goals that the building both symbolized and strove to embody; and (3) enabled an integrated building project and organization growth timeline that together readied the museum for its relocation, reopening, and new normal.

Our last strategic plan, approved by the Whitney's board of trustees in 2010, was written as a ten-year plan, the first five years of which would take us to our relocation and new building opening in May 2015. As part of the strategic planning process, senior staff were recast as a single strategic planning group; cross-departmental working groups were formed to implement the plan; and my role, as the Whitney's first-ever chief planning officer, was created to lead implementation efforts, parse priorities, and guide development of functional and departmental business plans and roadmaps. In 2012, two years into the plan and three years before our building opening, we revisited and recalibrated the plan's priorities. Our subsequent recalibration schedule included biweekly senior staff meetings and semiannual senior staff retreats—a cadence that our senior management group continues to follow today.

As we moved closer to the opening of our new building, we used the 2010 strategic plan more as a compass than as a roadmap, and we gradually shifted attention from "strategic planning priorities" to a timeline-dependent, laser focus on "critical path" priorities. This shift, as much psychological as procedural, ensured that operational and tactical activities mapped to the strategic plan and that the full, synchronized attention of the institution was necessarily on launching our new operation.

Even with a sound and iterative management framework for planning and prioritizing, our relocation and opening experienced both expected and unexpected highs and lows—

from critical accolades and a constant flow of visitors, to situational crises demanding rapid response from nearly all departments in the institution. Looking back, our first year of operation witnessed deep and unsettling change. With the challenge of addressing these fundamental changes—to location, environment, systems, ways of working, and people—as well as the substantial growth in our operation, Whitney staff had their hands full. Beyond staff, the museum's board of trustees had just closed out the largest capital campaign in our history (and among the largest capital campaigns by a museum or cultural institution in the country, to date). Capacity and fatigue of staff and volunteers were and still are real issues.

Change events, by definition, disrupt an organization's alignment and need to be addressed by leadership and strategists to achieve realignment. Indeed, after May 2015, much was different within the Whitney organization. Our physical transformation may have looked complete on the outside, but we still had work to do on the internal transformation. We were out of whack and needed, at minimum, an operational adjustment. Yet despite this, it was hard for anyone to fathom undertaking another strategic planning effort while in the throes of our first year.

We first looked at the 2010 strategic plan to understand whether an adjustment or a fresh start was preferable. After an evaluation by and discussion with our strategic planning group of senior staff, we realized that the realignment needs were not just operational but strategic. Prior to our relocation, we could not accurately predict or even envision our future state, regardless of tried-and-true planning tools available to us. (I think of the metaphor of the mountain climber who cannot even see the peak of the next, much larger mountain until atop the first.) After much discussion, we decided to "close out" our 2010 plan and start with a framework that better represented the needs and aspirations of the Whitney's new future. As challenging as it was to think about taking up a major strategic planning effort, we knew that it was the right decision.

And now for my second point: planning from a position of strength. Anyone who has re-located, opened a new building, closed out a major capital campaign, or dealt with mass staff turnover might agree that our new circumstances required a new strategic plan, but you still might ask: Why didn't we wait to launch a new strategic planning process until we were more settled? We certainly could have given ourselves an "opening-year pause" while we established our true operational baseline. While I believed that the shelf life of our 2010 strategic plan had expired once we opened our new building to the public in May 2015, there were many in the Whitney organization who disagreed. And even I would be hard pressed to argue that anyone on staff—especially the management team—had the time or capacity for a significant planning effort in our opening year.

So why didn't we wait during the intense, busy, overwhelming first year of new normal? Very simply, we chose to plan, proactively, from our new position of strength. We weighed the risk that our position would never be so strong, our vision never so ambitious, our staff and board never so confident as right now, and we acted fast to capitalize on the timing. Here, I will describe a few "strength factors" to consider and pose several critical questions to ask yourselves and your organization when you consider the best time to obtain the vast benefits of strategic planning.

Strength Factor 1: Confidence

Both the presence and nature of confidence in an organization are critical in a decision to undertake proactive strategic planning. I've chosen to address confidence first because I believe this to be a singularly underrated factor. Strategic planning is when you can and should take big risks with your thinking. Capturing a key leader, management team, set of stakeholders, or organizational culture at a time of confidence can make all the difference between a treading-water acceptance of incrementalism and big, beautiful leaps forward. Questions to ask include the following:

- Is your organization confident? Are you? If so, can you identify the sources of confidence? Can these be strengths to leverage?

- Can you look out twenty years and see a multitude of futures for your organization? Can anyone? Do you have aspirational thinkers among your leadership, staff, volunteers, and stakeholders?

- What has been your organization's greatest accomplishment in its last ten years? In its history? Does the answer to this question give you confidence? Or concern?

- Does your board have confidence in your organization? In the management team? Is this something you can leverage?

Strength Factor 2: Momentum

I want to provide a few examples, from the Whitney's experience, of the importance of momentum—both leveraging it when you have it and manufacturing it when you don't—in the process of strategic planning. For years prior to 2010, we had been working on strategic planning in fits and starts. But with no galvanizing set of events or goals in sight, planning petered out. In 2009, with strategic planning reactivated around our building project, we found ourselves in the midst of the financial crisis and poised to watch another strategic and building planning effort go by the wayside. Smartly, borrowing from the fundraising world, the Whitney mapped out and rallied around a series of milestones, including commissioning a series of large-scale works on the site of our new downtown home and, a year later, hosting a weeklong celebration of our "groundbreaking" breaking-ground ceremony. These milestones gave momentum and urgency to committing our thinking and resources to a new and better Whitney. At one point we even flirted with a "momentum committee" comprising staff and board members. While this may be taking the idea too far, that we considered it at all should demonstrate how critical a factor and powerful a tool momentum can be in strategic planning. If you think it might be time for strategic planning, ask the following questions:

- Is there momentum in the current environment? Which direction is it going and at what pace? Can you keep it going and for how long?

- Is there anything on the horizon that could help provide a tailwind? If not, what would it take to create something?

- Could you replicate a tailwind event or create "mini-milestones"?

- Could you manufacture urgency if you had to? How would you do this?

- Conversely, could you build momentum by leveraging forces of dissatisfaction or discussion of critical issues?

- What forces will constitute headwinds? Can your organization push through?

- Are there competing demands or projects that will steal valuable time, attention, thunder, or all of the above?

- Is there something driving the effort? Is there someone? Could there be? Who?

Strength Factor 3: Motivation

Motivation is an interesting concept, absent a trigger event. Unlike momentum, it is impossible to manufacture motivation. But once motivation has been spotted, it can be harnessed. Like momentum, motivation begets motivation. An open, transparent strategic planning process, as this book advocates, is important in generating and sustaining sufficient motivation from start to finish. Our most recent experience at the Whitney underlines this point. Despite intense fatigue from our first year of a greatly scaled-up operation and the net effect of staff turnover, more than a quarter of our entire staff directly engaged in new, cross-functional strategic planning committees assigned with dreaming up the Whitney's future. We found that once everyone aligned on strategic planning as the right decision, we could use our shared experience over our first year, both the highs and lows, as positive motivation to plan well for the years ahead. You might think about these questions:

- Is there a shared vision, goal, or common experience among staff and volunteers? Could there be? What would it take to get there? Could staff, volunteers, and stakeholders be motivated by the idea of seeking a shared vision together?

- If you asked "why now," would the answers present themselves to staff and volunteers clearly and easily? If not, what would it take to get there?

- Who are the motivators in your organization (management team, staff, and volunteers)? Can you count on their leadership and participation, start to finish?

- Are there motivators (stakeholders) outside your organization who can help?

- Can you sustain motivation for strategic planning long enough to complete the planning process?

Strength Factors 4 and 5: Management Team and Money

In defining a "position of strength," these last two factors seem obvious. Even if your organization is sound, solid, and solvent, you still might want to spend some time thinking through the following questions when launching a strategic planning process:

- Is this your or your CEO's top priority? Could it be?

- Is the rest of senior management on board?

- Can they carry the torch (is it the right group)? Are there leaders, not just senior managers?

- Would you know how to supplement your management team (staff, stakeholders, consultants, and others) if you had to?

- Do your management team and board have a good working relationship? Is communication clear and consistent?

- What is your organization's financial state? Is there (or could there also be) sufficient financial capacity to respond to small or large changes in direction?

- Does your board give? Would they invest in a new vision, if it came to that?

- What about other "investing" groups (patrons, donors, institutions, agencies)? What is your relationship with these investors?

- What other forms of financing are potentially available to you?

- How are your internal financial planning and budgeting processes? Your controls?

Figure 2.1 View of the new Whitney Museum of American Art from the High Line. *Image credit: MusikAnimal.*

Recognizing that not every organization can count on a building project like the Whitney's 2015 relocation to drive change and create urgency and realizing that major change events, both positive and negative or disruptive, will continue to drive the need for responsive strategic planning, I encourage organizations to think about strategic planning at high points in their lifecycle to capitalize on the lift generated by planning from a position of strength. I hope that our last two strategic planning experiences at the Whitney illustrate some of these key ideas.

Case Study 2.2

A New Strategic Direction for the Schomburg Center for Research in Black Culture

Joy Bailey-Bryant

The Schomburg Center for Research in Black Culture, a research unit of the New York Public Library, was established in 1925 as a unique reference collection of ten thousand items from the personal collection of Arturo Alfonso Schomburg. It is recognized across the globe as the leading research library and cultural center devoted exclusively to collecting, preserving, providing access to, and interpreting research resources on the global black experience. It is the inspiration for African and diasporan nations and communities exploring research, educational, and cultural centers and has been the model for three or four public institutions in the United States dedicated to this field, as well as two international institutions. The center set the standard for African American and African diasporic cataloguing nomenclature.

Entering its eighth decade of service to the nation and the world, the Schomburg had reached a crossroads. Like many libraries, it did not have its own operating board of trustees. As a research unit of the New York Public Library (NYPL), it was governed by the NYPL board and leadership. The NYPL and the Schomburg had recently completed negotiations to clarify the operational relationship—ensuring that the Schomburg remained autonomous in its collecting and preservation roles.

However, unlike branch libraries, the Schomburg was a research facility with no circulating collection—so no one could check out books—and its core audience was scholars who primarily lived outside Harlem. It was becoming clear that people passing by its doors every day—the geographic community—had likely never been inside the building and almost certainly had no idea what the center did or why it was important to the community.

Added to this, the Schomburg was facing increasing competition for collections: African American and African diasporic art, literature, and ephemera. When Arturo Schomburg began collecting at the height of the Harlem Renaissance, these items were considered a curiosity. Though Harlem Renaissance contributors—such as Zora Neale Hurston, Langston Hughes, Countee Cullen, and Jean Toomer—were celebrated, their works were saved in very few places. Ninety years later, the story was very different. In efforts to strengthen their research capacity, large and well-funded universities were actively seeking and purchasing entire collections from artists, writers, and thinkers. As a public library, the Schomburg could not compete with the funds that many universities were putting into their efforts. However, it was invested in maintaining its collections and keeping them accessible to populations that would never attend those schools.

Finally, the organization's "chief" for over twenty years had announced his retirement, and a successor had not been identified.

In this time of anticipated transition, identifying a clear strategic direction was imperative. Where would the center grow next? How would it tackle the collection issues and the ever-present nonprofit fiscal challenges?

In the absence of a governing board to assess and discuss the critical issues and opportunities and then set a direction, the leadership at the center decided to conduct a strategic planning process featuring benchmarking, an in-depth environmental scan, a robust internal and external analysis that led to the identification of critical issues, and a "convening" with world-class thinkers.

The center leveraged its international reputation to gather a panel of twenty of the brightest minds in twenty-first-century learning, technology, performing arts, museology, and library science. Participants included the founder of a popular website connecting people of color, the current "dean" of African American history, the leader of education for the Smithsonian, and the head of the New York Public Library.

This strategic visions convening was framed by a critical issues and opportunities paper that identified five key questions:

- What is the role of the Schomburg as a museum versus a library? What is the relationship between the Schomburg and the branch libraries?

- What is the future of marketing for the Schomburg? How does the Schomburg market its intellectual content?

- How does the Schomburg grow its digital presence?

- What are the qualities—knowledge, skills, and abilities—needed to lead this institution into the coming decades?

The panel also tackled "ancillary issues" that would have direct impact on the Schomburg in the future, such as the relationship of the Schomburg to gentrification with respect to cultural diversity in Harlem.

Strategic Directions for the Schomburg

The process resulted in a strategic directions document that became a roadmap, guiding the leadership in the design and development of a renewed Schomburg Center for the twenty-first century. The resulting recommendations were built around what a participant called, "the three Cs: collections, community, and conscience."

1. *Strengthen the Schomburg's reputation as a leading repository of the legacy of black people.* At the center of the Schomburg are its collections, which should be broadly disseminated to create a cultural milieu. The culture of the Schomburg must remain present while also asking what constituents want. The Schomburg's special collections on black history are its primary asset.

2. *Continue to build and expand the Shomburg's brand recognition locally, nationally, and internationally.* Among its existing audience, the Schomburg brand is recognized as a leading authoritative source of knowledge on the global black experience. However, the Schomburg should not overestimate its brand. There are 3.5 million people of African descent in New York City, and most of them do not know about the existence of the Schomburg. *One of the central distinguishing characteristics of a library is its sense of place*—a place where people come together. The center should therefore focus on becoming a destination for dynamic intellectual, cultural, entertainment, and learning experiences. *Recognizing that the exhibition and dissemination of the materials collected in research libraries is an emerging field*, new and developing institutions have significant square footage devoted to exhibitions and public programming.

3. *Realign staff and resources to better serve remote users while continuing to provide state-of-the-art services to on-site users.* The Schomburg must democratize while remaining a dedicated research space appealing to a new and younger public so that the functions of research libraries are clear to them. By expanding its digital presence, increasing production of online exhibits and products, and offering digital access to full-text collections, images, and audio-visual resources, the Schomburg can become the leading institution of black history on the Internet.

Today, the Schomburg is a renewed place. As a result of the strategic directions convening and resulting document, the NYPL hired noted scholar Khalil Gibran Muhammad to lead the institution. Under his leadership, the Schomburg has added more than nine thousand square feet and made other changes to serve community needs:

- a complete renovation of the Schomburg's second-floor reading room and an expansion of its rare book collection vault

- a new interactive gallery space for youth and teens, and compact storage for the Moving Image and Recorded Sound Division and the Art and Artifacts Division

- LED street signage, video displays, and artifact vitrines visible on the street, bringing Schomburg's programming and collections into the Harlem community, and expansion and relocation of the center's popular gift shop, which will move to the front of the building on the ground floor

- streetscape and landscape improvements—sidewalk paving, benches, and landscaping—to give New Yorkers a quiet space to congregate and view the screens and outdoor exhibitions

The museum aspects of the library are going strong—and so are efforts to publicize use of the collections. The Schomburg's attendance is among the top five African American museums, and it is among the top three tourist destinations in Harlem.

In 2014, the center gathered over a hundred research librarians from African American and African diasporic collections to discuss the state of the collection. The center also launched a film initiative encouraging cinematographers and documentarians to utilize its collections in their work. The results have been films such as *Shirley Chisholm, Unbought and Unbossed*, a film on the first African American woman to run for president, and *Harlem on my Plate*, a documentary on the culinary styles of Harlem.

Figure 2.2 Participants in the Schomburg's Junior Scholars Program gather in the Langston Hughes lobby. The program is one of many designed to cultivate younger audiences as outlined in the Strategic Directions goals. One hundred youth from the New York City area, ages eleven to eighteen, are selected each year for this precollege black studies program. *Image credit: Schomburg Center for Research in Black Culture.*

Chapter 3

Who and What

The Structure of Strategic Planning

Strategic planning is the joint responsibility of the governing body and staff leadership. There are relatively few aspects of managing cultural nonprofits that are shared by the board and staff—that is why strategic planning can be both difficult and dangerous.

Strategic planning can be difficult because, generally, formal communication between board and staff takes place through the director unless the director has designated a senior manager for a particular committee—anything else could be considered either "meddling" by the board or "insubordination" by the staff. This clear separation of governance and management has been one of the major achievements of the struggle to professionalize cultural organizations over the past fifty years. In the now-traditional model of nonprofit cultural governance, a board deals with policy and fundraising, and a staff operates the cultural organization in accordance with board policy as interpreted by the director. The director and board chair work very closely together—indeed, they are key partners in steering the institution. In some organizations, staff members are invited to observe board meetings, but that is usually the limit of communication apart from socializing at openings and special events.

Strategic planning can be risky because it turns the tables and brings the governing body and staff together to talk about issues, to resolve challenges, and to plan the future together. Making this a productive and creative process (rather than a meddlesome, quarrelsome one) requires a clear structure with limits and accountability.

Leadership

Leadership in the strategic planning process is provided by the director of the organization and the chair of the governing body working with a steering committee. The director and board chair collaborate with each other; the director leads the staff, and the board chair leads the governing body through the process.

In the past, it was customary when strategic planning time rolled around for the director, board chair, and a few close advisors to sequester themselves for a weekend and write the strategic plan. The plan would then be reviewed by executive staff, the financials would be added, it would be presented to the board for adoption, and finally the plan would be rolled out to staff for implementation. This approach is quick and relatively painless. However, the two main disadvantages are that the strategy is not owned by the staff who are charged to implement it and that it does not benefit from the insights of stakeholders and communities who support the institution.

Today, cultural organizations look outward, focused on their roles in society, and that is why the strategic planning process as described in this manual is inclusive.

Once the governing body and senior management have determined that a new strategic plan is needed, the first step is for the director and board chair to appoint a strategic planning steering committee. The steering committee should comprise six to twelve people (including the director and board chair) with slightly more board than staff representation. At the end of the process, the governing body approves the strategic plan; if the governing body does not have confidence in the plan (which means that it is committed to advocate for it and fund its implementation), the entire effort will have been a failure.

There is no recipe for composing a steering committee. As you consider candidates, use the following checklists:

Board Members of the Steering Committee

- Will they make time to attend steering committee meetings?

- Are they respected by board colleagues?

- Do they reflect the diversity of the board in terms of gender, age, race, new trustees, long-standing trustees, and outlook?

- Are they are enthusiastic about strategic planning?

- Will they report to the full governing body on the progress of the plan?

- Will they keep information shared within the steering committee confidential?

- Are they team players?

Special consideration needs to be given to board participation in organizations that are departments of larger bodies such as municipalities and universities. In these cases, the immediate advisory board plays the larger role. The governing body might appoint one representative to the process.

Staff Members of the Steering Committee

- Will they make time to attend steering committee meetings?

- Are they respected by colleagues?

- Do they reflect the diversity of the staff in terms of gender, age, race, length of service, perspective, and level of responsibility?

- Will they represent the good of the entire institution rather than lobby for a particular department?

- Are they enthusiastic about strategic planning?

- Will they report to all-staff meetings on the progress of the plan?

- Will they keep information shared within the steering committee confidential?

- Are they are team players?

The director and board chair are usually cochairs of the steering committee. However, another board member might serve as cochair because the job will continue as the plan is reviewed and progress is charted during the plan's three- to five-year time frame.

The roles and responsibilities of the steering committee are as follows:

- Assess the effectiveness of the previous strategic plan and determine what should be different this time.

- Formulate and approve the strategic planning process.

- Retain the services of consultants if and as required.

- Guide the consultants or staff charged with conducting the plan.

- Engage board and staff in the process, especially the strategic planning retreat, as appropriate.

- Sign off on all draft documents that go to the board for approval.

- Support management's effort to prepare the new strategic plan while including input from the board and staff (especially from the retreat).

- Recommend the plan to the board for approval.

It is wise for the steering committee to appoint a coordinator to assist in necessary interactions, including the following:

- Schedule meetings and prepare minutes and agendas.

- Coordinate consultation processes and research.

- Compile reports.

- Distribute reports to the right people at the right time.

- Organize the logistics of the retreat and other events.

Facilitation

Professional consultants are often retained to assist in preparing strategic plans because a consultant brings an outside point of view, facilitation skills, and a broad perspective on cultural trends. However, many nonprofit cultural organizations cannot afford consultants. This should not discourage you from strategic planning. Indeed, the staff of cultural organizations have considerable expertise, and this book is intended to help your own staff facilitate and guide the strategic plan. It has been coauthored by a cultural planning consultant, who has facilitated numerous strategic plans in many cultural sectors, and by a museum director, who has facilitated strategic plans in museums that she has led—both with and without the assistance of consultants.

The key facilitation roles in strategic planning are

- planning and coordinating the entire process

- facilitating meetings and workshops

- moderating the retreat

- preparing background documents, research, and reports

- conducting confidential interviews

- coaching staff to write the strategic plan document

The director and board chair need to decide whether the organization has the staff resources and expertise to conduct some or all of these tasks. If external help is needed, those in charge need to decide whether the consultant should be a cultural specialist, a generalist strategic planner, an academic, or an expert on loan from a foundation or a corporation.

If a staff member performs the role of consultant, the individual needs to wear a "consultant hat" and make clear to colleagues that he or she is not representing the department in the process and will need support to complete his or her regular job.

Once these options have been reviewed, the strategic planning steering committee recommends the approach to be taken. Staff then prepare a request for proposals (RFP) for a paid consultant or create a position description for work done voluntarily by museum staff or pro bono by a university or other organization. Preparing a written description of the tasks to be accomplished is essential for the process to work.

When we use the term *consultant* in this book, we are referring to the role of consultant and facilitator, whether conducted by a professional consultant, a staff member, another advisor, or a combination of all of these.

The Ten Steps of Strategic Planning

This ten-step process has been found by the authors to be very effective in strategic planning for the full range of not-for-profit cultural organizations.

The process starts with two broad perspectives: the environmental scan (step 1) and external assessment (step 2). It then narrows through an internal analysis of your institution's strengths and weaknesses (step 3) and then narrows further as the steering committee determines the key issues facing your organization (step 4).

Step 5 is the "pinch point" in the diagram when the strategic planning retreat or workshop occurs—here the process is focused on resolving the key issues, determining the overarching goals for the next three to five years, and revising the foundation statements as needed. At this point the steering committee leads the process (even though a consultant often facilitates the retreat).

After the retreat, the process begins to broaden as staff members determine how each department will fulfill the goals and as the strategic plan is written. The broadest aspect is step 10: implementation and evaluation.

1. Environmental Scan Discussion Paper

Because strategic planning shows how organizations can be successful in the face of constant change, the first step in the process provides an occasion for everyone in an organization to discuss the effects of change. This is called an "environmental scan" because it describes at a high level how similar organizations have responded to the challenges of social, political, and cultural change. The environmental scan is an opportunity for the entire governing body and staff to learn from innovations in technology, diversity, regional growth and decline, competition for leisure time, the "knowledge economy," urbanization, immigration, and so forth.

The topics will vary from place to place and from organization to organization. For example, as indicated in chapter 1, libraries may be affected by digitization more than performing arts centers, but all organizations will be affected by the economy. Every discussion paper should include a concise section that reports on the organization's performance relative to that of its peers, both locally and nationally.

A good way to start off the environmental scan is to brainstorm with the steering committee to learn what they see as the key forces of change. The list that emerges can be developed through further research into an environmental scan discussion paper. This document, which should be both concise (no more than ten pages) and interesting, is circulated to everyone in the museum family (board, staff, and volunteers). To encourage discussion, the paper should pose questions.

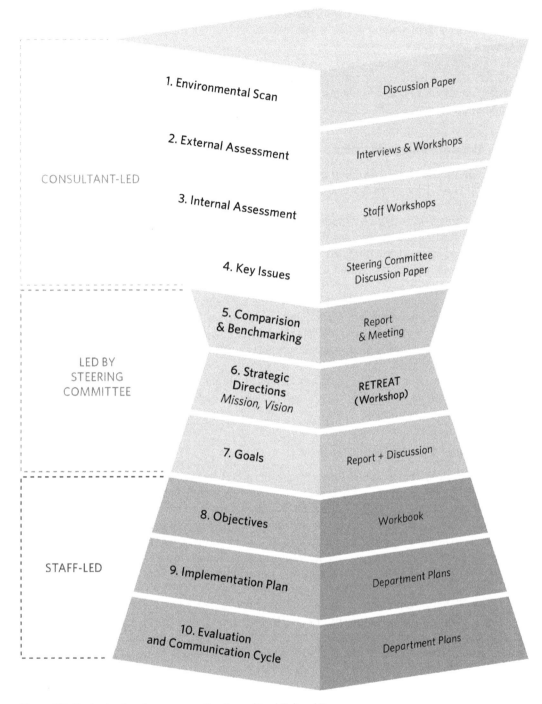

Figure 3.1 Strategic planning process. *Courtesy of Lord Cultural Resources.*

Manual of Strategic Planning for Cultural Organizations

Time should be taken in board meetings and staff workshops in step 2 to discuss these issues. The resulting ideas should be added to the findings in step 3.

The main objectives of preparing a discussion paper are to create a level playing field of information so that people of different backgrounds and interests can begin to communicate and to encourage big-picture thinking beyond narrow departmental and sectoral interests. Here are some examples of the discussions stimulated by environmental scans.

Library Staff Workshop

In the discussion paper, immigration from Latin America was identified as a community trend. In the staff discussions, librarians identified the relevance of music and DVD collections, program staff suggested holding family festivals and encouraging English as a second language classes to meet at the library, while security and cleaning staff pointed out that many of them are from Latin American countries and suggested the library regularly canvass their opinions before deciding on programs.

The staff member on the steering committee who was facilitating the meeting noted the ideas on a flip chart and said they would be included in the next report.

Museum Board Workshop

In the discussion paper, one of the trends noted was that many museums are forming national and international partnerships to share exhibitions and even collections. Board members were curious about how these partnerships work and debated whether their museum could create links with famous European museums to attract more publicity and community notice. Others asked if these international relations could make money.

Board members on the steering committee who presided over this workshop said they would take the questions back to the steering committee and get answers to include in the next report.

2. External Assessment

In order to determine its "best future," an organization needs to see itself as others see it. But, how many others and which others? These are questions of strategy, budget, and time. There are five categories of "others" to be consulted:

- opinion leaders

- community leaders

- visitors

- nonvisitors

- peers and experts

In all cases, the findings should be organized by general category, not by individuals, to maintain confidentiality and to receive full and frank opinions and perceptions.

The individuals being consulted need to know the purpose of the interview and how their input will be used. Their participation should be acknowledged with a thank-you letter and credit in the final strategic plan document.

3. Internal Assessment

Opinions about the organization's present performance and future direction should be gathered from within the museum—board, staff, volunteers, donors, and members.

Depending on scheduling and timing, the internal assessment can be step 2 or step 3, or both steps can take place at the same time. The internal assessment process is conducted as individual interviews (with board executives and senior staff members) and as facilitated discussions. The environmental scan should be circulated to all participants in advance of the consultation because it will help to stimulate new ways of thinking. These interviews and workshops usually proceed through a SWOT process—exploring the organization's strengths, weaknesses, opportunities, and threats.

How does one communicate the findings from all of these consultations? In order to obtain the full benefit of this input, the report must balance analysis with direct quotation and accurate paraphrasing. Having been consulted, the board and staff will definitely be looking at the findings report to see if their opinions were heard. Skeptics will be out to prove that their views were not heard. The same guidelines concerning the external assessment report also apply to the internal:

*   Report the findings by category of staff, board, volunteers, members, and donors.

*   Within each category, report on strengths, weaknesses, opportunities, and threats with a balanced introduction to each followed by quotations and paraphrases, with those most frequently mentioned by category at the top of the list and those least mentioned at the bottom.

Discuss the full report with the strategic planning steering committee and develop a broad summary based on that discussion, making the full report available on request or as an appendix.

4. Key Issues

During the data gathering and investigative phase of strategic planning (steps 1 through 3), scores, possibly hundreds, of issues will have emerged. However, in order to determine the optimal future for the organization, we need to understand—in some depth—the issues critical to its future.

> Key issues are those facing a cultural organization that, when addressed, will put it on track to be more successful.

All inputs need to be considered by the steering committee. The consultant or facilitator can reorganize the many issues from a report format (who said what) to an analytic format organized by theme or topic. Chapter 4 explains in more detail how strategic planning helps an organization move from a diffuse awareness of "problems" to a clear grasp on the key issues.

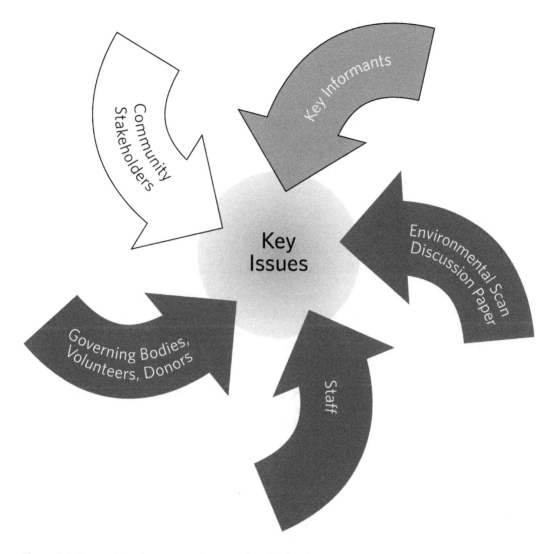

Figure 3.2 Determining key issues. *Courtesy of Lord Cultural Resources.*

The key issues discussion paper is the main document that is distributed in advance to participants in the strategic planning retreat or workshop.

5. Comparison and Benchmarking

Once the key issues have been identified, find out how other relevant institutions have addressed these issues. This could lead to a formal benchmarking study or a more informal approach whereby members of the steering committee contact colleagues and discuss how they addressed the issues, which strategies worked, and which didn't.

Benchmarking is a rigorous and thorough process of investigating how another organization has addressed similar issues.

Another approach is to invite experts to visit your organization and provide insights. In advance of the visit, the experts (who should be selected because of their insight and experience with the key issues) are provided the key issues discussion paper. They then participate in discussions with the steering committee, staff, and board. In one strategic plan that the authors worked on, the invited experts made presentations in public forums chaired by the director, which were broadcast on public radio.

6. Setting Strategic Directions

The director and board chair both play strong roles in the strategic planning process by serving as cochairs of the strategic planning committee and by guiding the plan's vision. With respect to strategic direction and vision, the director's role is decisive. The entire organization looks to the director for leadership. Some directors prepare a visionary strategic plan for discussion at the retreat, using the input from the previous stages. Other directors prefer a more inductive process whereby the retreat participants debate key issues identified by the strategic planning committee and then draft the strategy after the retreat. Both approaches can be equally effective. The choice is mainly a matter of leadership style and institutional culture.

The strategic planning retreat or workshop is a day devoted to establishing the optimal future for the organization and the changes required to achieve it. Chapter 6 describes how to organize the retreat and the processes for working out the strategic directions. The key outcomes of the day should include the following:

- a discussion that leads to prioritizing the "key issues"

- identification of strategic directions that will address these issues and move the organization forward decisively toward its optimal future

- a review of the organization's foundation statements (mission, vision, and mandate) to determine whether they express the museum's optimal future

Depending on how advanced the process is at this point, the retreat could also adopt goals for the next three to five years.

7. Establishing Goals

Goals, which are long range and qualitative, are distinct from *objectives*, which are short term and quantitative, and *tasks*, which are the particular steps needed to fulfill an objective. Goals are big and strategic—they take an institution toward a future direction. They are not "business as usual." For most cultural organizations, "business as usual" means fulfilling all the departmental functions described in chapter 1. Goals are crosscutting and interdepartmental; goals necessarily involve multiple functions and multiple departments.

However, what would constitute a goal leading to strategic change for one organization could be "business as usual" for another. Take, for example, an issue like "weak governance." For a performing arts center where the board lacks leadership, diversity, and a committee structure, a goal could be "to build board leadership in diversity, prestige, and financial capacity." For another center that has all its board mechanisms and committee structures functioning well, board development is "business as usual" and not a goal. There are no "standard" or "typical" goals—each organization must determine its own.

In some situations, the strategic planning retreat is the occasion to establish the strategic goals. In other situations—especially if the institution has never done an inclusive planning process—it may be advisable to defer the goal setting to the steering committee, which should meet soon after the retreat.

A concise retreat report is prepared to summarize the decisions of the retreat and the recommended goals for board approval. Responsibility for preparing this report must be clearly assigned before the retreat.

8. Objectives

Those keeping an eye on the hourglass diagram will notice at this point a widening of the diagram: once the goals have been established by the retreat or the steering committee, the focus shifts to management and staff to determine the best way to achieve these goals. In chapter 7, we introduce a workbook for departments to use to analyze current plans and objectives, to organize them around the new goals, and to add objectives (and tasks) where needed—indicating where additional resources will be required.

9. Implementation Plan

It is up to senior management to integrate departmental input into a coherent plan, eliminating duplication of effort, coordinating the achievement of goals through multidepartmental teams, and ensuring that all this activity can be accomplished within the budget. This often means raising additional money from government or private sources, on the one hand, or cutting or downsizing programs and projects that do not contribute to the strategic goals, on the other. Executive management has to scrutinize departmental plans and initiatives, combine and recombine them, create clear priorities, and use the agreed-upon strategic goals—by adding significant resources, by eliminating nonstrategic activities, or, more usually, by doing both. The implementation plan is then worked out with department heads, who amend their departmental plans. The finance team produces the budgetary plan and a critical path. An executive summary is written for general distribution. The implementation plan (and not the departmental plans) goes to the governing body for discussion, amendment, and approval.

10. Evaluation

One of the most common complaints about planning is that, after being completed, it "sat on the shelf" and was not implemented. Sometimes, the plan was *not* implemented; in other situations, the plan *was* implemented but neither board nor staff realized it. An ongoing evaluation process is an effective way of increasing awareness of the implementation process:

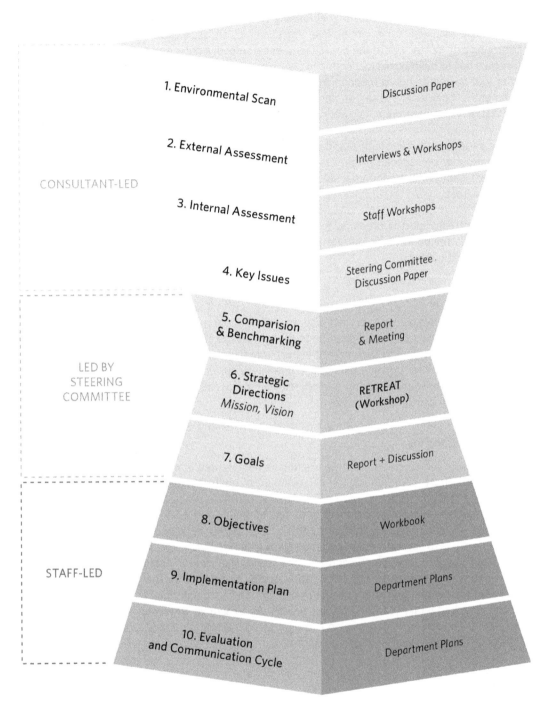

CONSULTANT-LED

1. Environmental Scan — Discussion Paper

2. External Assessment — Interviews & Workshops

3. Internal Assessment — Staff Workshops

4. Key Issues — Steering Committee Discussion Paper

LED BY STEERING COMMITTEE

5. Comparision & Benchmarking — Report & Meeting

6. Strategic Directions *Mission, Vision* — RETREAT (Workshop)

7. Goals — Report + Discussion

STAFF-LED

8. Objectives — Workbook

9. Implementation Plan — Department Plans

10. Evaluation and Communication Cycle — Department Plans

Figure 3.3 Staff-led strategic planning process (bottom of figure). *Courtesy of Lord Cultural Resources.*

- If there are five goals in the plan, the director should report on progress and problems for one or two goals at each senior staff meeting, each board meeting, and each all-staff meeting.

- Department heads should make their management reports under the headings of the five goals rather than by function, which is the usual report structure.

- The director should report strategic plan progress to the annual board meeting, addressing both successes and problems and recommending any needed changes.

- The annual report should include a section on progress toward achieving the strategic plan.

- The human resources department should include a section in all performance evaluations regarding how the employee contributed to the goals of the strategic plan.

- The revised mission or vision statement could be printed on all business cards.

- In addition, the strategic plan should be easily accessible to staff at all times on the organization's intranet.

One year before the conclusion of the plan, management should assess what has been accomplished and what has not, then should guide staff and the board in completing what needs to be completed—formally evaluating the strengths and weaknesses of the plan and determining whether conditions require a simple update using a few of the ten steps or a new full-scale effort using all ten steps.

Case Study 3.1

Tafelmusik's Strategic Plan for Acoustical Excellence

Tricia Baldwin

The quality of a concert hall is fundamental to the artistic and audience experience. It is the musicians' instrument, so to speak, and its design can empower a breathtaking communication of the greatest music ever written to audiences over the ages.

The internationally acclaimed Tafelmusik Baroque Orchestra had performed in the best concert halls in the world, yet the acoustic quality of its home venue in Toronto—a church—was inhibiting future artistic and audience growth. The home venue defines the sound of an ensemble, and improving Tafelmusik's home venue, where the fifty-performance home season took place, would make it possible for the orchestra to take its next artistic leap. Even on an annual budget of $5 million, Tafelmusik had always set and achieved bold goals on the world stage; this time, the goal was to create a "Stradivarius" of a hall in its home city for baroque music and beyond.

The strengths of this venue improvement initiative were involving the artistic team, board of directors, project partners, and key stakeholders at all phases; focusing the project on the core artistic and audience mandate; incorporating venue improvements into the strategic plan as a top priority; commissioning extensive architectural, engineering, and fundraising research by the top practitioners in the field; extensively evaluating the artistic, audience, operations, and financial implications of four options in order to choose the best strategic and artistic direction; developing a plethora of risk-management strategies, clearly managing expectations and processes through a professional tendering process and defining them in legal contracts; ensuring governance and control of the project management process during the implementation phase; and truly appreciating the many people that brought a remarkable dream to fruition. It does get down to the quality of people, vision, and mission. The integrity and importance of the initiative and its players, the determination and fortitude of leadership, and the belief in and nurturing of close partnerships all enable great things to happen and allow storms to be weathered along the way.

Tafelmusik, with its wonderful partners at its home venue of Trinity-St. Paul's Centre, set upon a decade-long journey of discovery that enabled the orchestra and choir to perform in acoustically excellent venues in their home city of Toronto while continuing to bring their music to the world through touring and recording.

Focus on Mission

The mission of the Tafelmusik Baroque Orchestra and Chamber Choir was to be a national and international center of musical excellence in period performance for generations to come. Tafelmusik's mandate was reflected in the following artistic pillars, in order of importance: (1) major home season; (2) provincial, national, and international touring; (3) recording; (4) artist training; and (5) education. Given that Tafelmusik's top priority was its home season, improving its home venue was essential. The orchestra wanted to bring its home audience the level of excellence it was able to achieve in the best halls in the world.

Many nonprofit organizations dabble in "mission creep"—that is, they stray from their core mission with interesting projects that are irrelevant to the mandate. In the case of Tafelmusik, the improvement of its home venue was at the very heart of its vision, mission, and mandate, which is why the organization moved mountains to achieve its goal.

For three decades, since 1981, Tafelmusik's beloved home venue was Trinity-St. Paul's United Church (TSP). Arts, faith, and social justice groups happily coexisted in this warm and intimate heritage space, which was a perfect environment for period chamber orchestra and choir concerts. This venue was Tafelmusik's golden egg, as the sharing of music between the dynamic musicians and loving audience in this church was something to behold. Its affordability had enabled Tafelmusik to punch above its weight on the world stage through extensive touring and recording. Unfortunately, TSP had suboptimal acoustics and audience comfort, and the building was ailing.

Examining Strategic Options

A Tafelmusik building committee was started with musicians, staff, and board members; TSP created a building management board; and a joint committee of TSP and Tafelmusik was also established. Despite a sometimes arduous and dramatic process that would make even a Puccini opera appear dispassionate, the focus on delivering a world-class concert hall for a world-class orchestra did not waver during the ten years leading up to the renovations.

The tumultuous part of any transformative project is the period of setting sail on ambiguous waters to seek information and answers. The resulting discomfort produces a force of equal and opposite magnitude as various parties express a desire to make decisions prematurely in order to return to solid ground again. As a leader, it is important to ensure that the organization has done its due diligence not only with the capital project itself, but also with its long-term impact on operations. Time, research, and a deep and broad process are needed for the future health and vibrancy of the organization itself.

Tafelmusik examined four options. First, maintain the status quo—do nothing. Second, purchase TSP, invest $25 million in a grand revovation, and get into the business of venue ownership and operations. Third, move completely to the Royal Conservatory of Music's Koerner Hall, an excellent new 1,135-seat hall down the street. Or, fourth, engage in a hybrid strategy: complete more modest leasehold improvements of TSP without ownership, at a cost of $3 million, and perform some of the series concerts at Koerner Hall.

Various attempts at major public funding were made but nothing materialized, making the second option untenable. It was not until a more modest, leasehold improvement project was presented that the real possibility of government funding became apparent. Moreover, Tafelmusik did not want to get into the business of venue ownership and operations when so much attention was required for its home season, touring, recording, and education programs. Thus, although it was important to think big, the grander option was deemed impractical and undesirable.

Given the two-year terms for board chair, there were five Tafelmusik board chairs during this process, and they held divergent opinions at various stages—some were enthusiastic about the Koerner Hall model and others were enthusiastic about venue ownership. The artistic and audience experience in Koerner Hall was unknown until it opened in 2009, so, rather than continuing to debate the issue, the organization waited until it had opened and was tested by the orchestra. It is a beautiful venue, but the artistic team determined it to be most suitable for larger works of their baroque and classical repertoire on period instruments. Furthermore, this new venue's popularity resulted in limited access, which made it unsuitable as a full-time venue for Tafelmusik's large home concert season, the schedule of which worked around international tours, Opera Atelier engagements, and recordings. Koerner Hall's cost structure, even with the discount that was kindly provided, would have prohibited Tafelmusik's ability to tour internationally and record at the extensive level it had for decades. From artistic, logistical, scheduling, and financial perspectives, full-time occupancy at Koerner Hall was not deemed an option.

Strategic Choice

Tafelmusik's building committee reconvened in 2010 and developed the "hybrid" plan that enabled it to reach new audiences with its larger repertoire projects at the excellent new Koerner Hall while maintaining its beloved and intimate 750-seat TSP home. This option included making acoustical, audience, safety, accessibility, equipment, and aesthetic leasehold improvements of TSP. Tafelmusik's building committee collaborated with TSP's building management board and general manager. The building program was developed with ERA Architects and acclaimed acoustician Bob Essert of Sound Space Design, and approval was given by all parties involved.

Risk Management

The Tafelmusik board had agreed to the building committee's recommendation to undertake this venue project, and they donated generously in support of it because they knew the importance of venue improvement and diversification for artistic and audience development. This was a board with considerable financial acuity, and their key governance concern was risk management. The board created a project oversight committee that worked hand in hand with the management and finance committee during the renovations planning and implementation period. Cost risk management was addressed in the planning period with architectural feasibility research and studies, extensive structural and electrical engineering studies, numerous cost estimate studies at each stage of the planning, significant budget contingencies, detailed project management, budget planning and forecasting overseen by the board of directors, and the ability to limit the scope of renovations by completing the project in phases based on private and public sector revenues actually earned for the project. During the implementation period, risk management was addressed through project management dashboards that showcased any risk areas, biweekly forecasts and meetings with the contractor, and financial limits placed on signing authority for change orders.

Figure 3.4 Tafelmusik's renewed concert hall at Trinity-St. Paul's Centre, Toronto. *Courtesy of Virtuo 360.*

Figure 3.5 The writer and director inspecting the renovations in progress. *Courtesy of Martin Reis.*

Risk management on the revenue side was addressed with an independent capital fundraising feasibility study, donor research and identification, prospect development, and collaboration among members of the staff, artists, and board team and major donors. Tafelmusik had not yet established a major gift program, so it had to set up from scratch a system that would track research, cultivation, acquisition, and stewardship of gifts from $25,000 to $1 million. With assistance from outside fundraising counsel and a focus on the major gift program implementation, a leadership gift was provided by an individual donor in honor of Tafelmusik's music director, Jeanne Lamon. Modest requests for federal and municipal public funding were granted, given proof that Tafelmusik had matching funds in hand as required by these government programs.

Tafelmusik had rid itself of its deficit years before and had systematically put surplus funds aside each year; those funds provided a buffer for unexpected financial surprises during this priority project. These excess funds also eased cash-flow management during peak times of the renovation.

The Outcome

Music critic Robert Harris wrote, "If a hall is the orchestra's instrument, Tafelmusik has just traded the violin that your mom bought you for an Amati, if not a Stradivarius." The musicians were both astonished and moved by the beautiful sound in their home venue. After the preview concert for subscribers, Tafelmusik had expected comments about how much more comfortable the seats were, but instead received a deluge of comments by people moved to tears by how beautiful the sound was. It was all about the music and the vision: serve the art form and the artists, and they can then serve the audience.

With the improved concert and lobby space, Trinity-St. Paul's was able to achieve a more sustainable operation with increased performance-related rental revenues to cover operations and maintenance of its heritage building, something that was also in the interest of its performing arts partners. This was a win-win strategy for all parties who had dedicated thousands of hours to the project over a decade.

The extensive research into strategic venue options paid off, as the optimal strategic direction that emerged was a combination of the alternatives. The improvement of the cherished Trinity-St. Paul's Centre and the expansion into Koerner Hall for several larger programs afforded Tafelmusik outstanding acoustics in both venues and the ability to expand audience reach and participation significantly.

Case Study 3.2

Benefits of Strategic Planning in Science Centers

Kathleen Brown

In 2011, the TELUS Spark Science Centre in Calgary, Alberta, was transformed into a purpose-built science center responding to the need for twenty-first-century skills development through inquiry-based and design-thinking learning. The new 153,000 square-foot science center had a new name and five new interactive galleries housing more than 120 exhibits. But it was facing some new challenges as well.

As the institution continued to evolve, a new capital funding opportunity spurred an initiative to understand and analyze several different opportunities within the context of a broader strategic vision. Should TELUS Spark consider a preschool or day care operation? How can it serve the growing tech industry in Calgary? How can it best support informal science education, and what are the facility implications? How should the current "maker movement" inform or shape aspects of the visitor experience and program? Are events and food service important opportunities? To answer these questions, TELUS Spark's leadership decided to engage in a comprehensive strategic plan.

Some Fundamental Challenges Facing Science Centers

TELUS Spark senior staff members began preparing for the strategic planning process by holding exploratory sessions to better understand the need for and viability of several business initiatives. In the strategic planning context, conversations with outside science center professionals and benchmarking data can be a "game changer" because the knowledge shared leads to a much broader contextual understanding of what is realistic and reasonable with respect to institutional histories, norms, patterns, and performance parameters. For TELUS Spark, this contextual analysis grounded the strategic planning process on the front end.

The environmental scan revealed that TELUS's key issues are shared by other science centers. The majority of science centers today rely too heavily on earned revenues and are unable to quantify and communicate their social impact. Discussions among the TELUS Spark senior staff, board leadership, outside science center professionals, and consultants revealed new information that helped staff contextualize, scrutinize, and validate their own perspectives, adding further depth and nuance to their understanding of their situation.

TELUS Spark is at the forefront as a twenty-first-century learning institution with innovative programs and activities. During initial staff workshops, the staff noted that the organization needed to link programming and activities more fully with the organizational strategy. The strategic planning process was a welcome solution; the process would help staff understand which programs and activities should be retained and which should be abandoned moving forward. This benefit would also positively affect internal communication and enhance efficiencies. The cross-functional nature of the strategic planning process sparked dialogue and collaboration between staff and departments and enhanced institution-wide teamwork. These interpersonal impacts encouraged synergy and holistic decision making, promoting alignment around newly held aspirations.

The partnership between the board and staff also benefits from the strategic planning process—finding common ground and alignment through shared discovery and learning is a powerful experience. In particular, discussing the history and evolution of science centers as part of the environmental scan stimulated thinking about external partnerships, community engagement, and the need to further define and investigate meaningful key performance indicators. Such conversations provide context to the board and senior staff so that they can better understand where their own institution is at the present time, the decisions or plans that led it to that point, and the potential directions for the institution in the future.

Evolution of Science Centers

Science centers are a relatively new type of institution that has evolved in four stages or "waves."

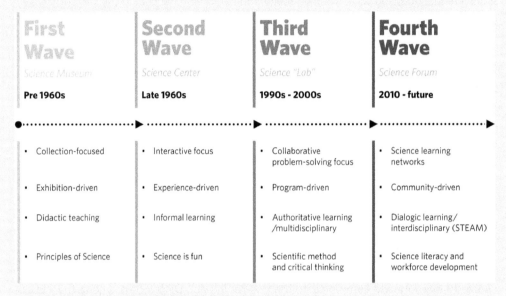

First Wave	Second Wave	Third Wave	Fourth Wave
Science Museum	Science Center	Science "Lab"	Science Forum
Pre 1960s	**Late 1960s**	**1990s - 2000s**	**2010 - future**
• Collection-focused	• Interactive focus	• Collaborative problem-solving focus	• Science learning networks
• Exhibition-driven	• Experience-driven	• Program-driven	• Community-driven
• Didactic teaching	• Informal learning	• Authoritative learning /multidisciplinary	• Dialogic learning/ interdisciplinary (STEAM)
• Principles of Science	• Science is fun	• Scientific method and critical thinking	• Science literacy and workforce development

Figure 3.6 A brief history of science centers. *Courtesy of Lord Cultural Resources.*

The characteristics of the four waves are identified in the diagram, some attributes of which are consistent with the parallel trajectory of other educational and cultural organizations. Newer science centers such as TELUS Spark typically emerge within the third or fourth waves. The chart shows that the "new" TELUS Spark of 2011 was actually at the very beginning of the fourth wave—but the organization was functioning as a third-wave science center.

The following questions can help all science centers better understand their position in the fast-moving world of science centers:

• Where does our institution fall within the broad sweep of science center development? Where would we like to be?

• Which of the characteristics or trends within these waves will affect us most in the coming years?

• What characteristics are most important to us? What makes us unique within the context of these developments? How can we capitalize on our strengths?

- How does our vision align with where we actually are? What changes need to be made to better reflect our aspirations?

These discussions brought new understanding to TELUS Spark board members who participated in them. One insight was related to the role of science centers in civil society: How do we help people evaluate facts and become discerning consumers and synthesizers of scientific information? This facilitated conversation set a new standard for engaged dialogue that will reverberate in the planning process and beyond—especially through an ongoing, conscious effort to invite and make time for these discussions at future board meetings.

Understanding the Needs of Visitors and Communities

The consultants' research brought to the discussion an external perspective that raised awareness of broader community needs and expectations. The initial research also indicated some potential areas of endeavor and clarified the need for further investigations: What are our core competencies? What are the community's needs and how do we clarify what we measure to ensure we meet them? How do we know which program ideas are the best fit?

Through the consultation process, two key audience segments—preschoolers and science teachers—were identified as central to future development. As a young, growing city with an increasingly important science and technology sector, Calgary is underserved with meaningful and vibrant preschool programs. The opportunity became apparent to TELUS Spark's staff, who then explored the viability of an in-center preschool program in partnership with a childcare provider. With the growing importance of the science and technology sector in the city and the need for a science-literate workforce, the vision of promoting "science-ready" students entering school at the very beginning of their formal learning journey has real traction.

Similarly, TELUS Spark is uniquely positioned to provide science teachers with the tools and training to support students in their formal learning. Through workshops with teachers, the center's informality, spontaneity, and experience that makes science fun and memorable for students is what appeals to science teachers. In many cases, these qualities can be integrated into lesson plans so that visits to the science center are not "one-off" events but build a seamless and conscious continuum of experience that leads to a lifelong love of science learning. This is manifestly present in Calgary, which is the home of the Open Minds / Campus Calgary program, in which a class of students spends up to one week on-site at a local cultural institution; TELUS Spark is a core participant in this program.

Further, in light of the growing technology sector in Calgary and western Canada in general, TELUS Spark senior staff perceived the potential for professional development and team-building opportunities for local corporations seeking to promote a high-functioning workforce. In this way, TELUS Spark seeks to develop core activities that will strategically affect key market segments and influencers: children just entering school (and their parents), science teachers across the school-age spectrum, and the growing technology-sector employer base (and their employees).

TELUS Spark is also studying their visitors' interactions with on-floor "maker labs" to better understand those opportunities and how they achieve their intended impacts (love of science and technology, comfort with hands-on learning). Understanding and addressing needs programmatically and matching those needs to the institution's capabilities and core attributes through its exhibitions can help the science center fulfill its mission.

Clarity for Funders and Supporters

Like TELUS Spark, many science centers came into existence because of a perceived need for informal science experiences. One of the key issues facing many science centers right now is a crisis of confidence: What is our unique value proposition in the context of myriad opportunities for science learning—through media, "edutainment," and the Internet? How do we best leverage the investments we make in physical facilities, resource-intensive exhibitions, and escalating operating costs to maximize social impact? How do we balance all of our activity and revenue streams to achieve our best and highest potentials? These are exactly the questions and issues of balance that TELUS Spark will continue to examine as its strategic planning process unfolds over the course of its life cycle.

The proportion of private or contributed funding in the revenue mix of science centers tends to fall well below that achieved by other cultural institutions for a variety of complex reasons. As a result, science centers are under intense pressure to generate increasing levels of earned revenue. TELUS Spark's experience is consistent with this general pattern, as it generates ten times more earned revenue than contributed revenue. Science center business models are frequently overwhelmed by initiatives created to support their educational mission in tangential ways, and these efforts become the operational equivalent of the "tail wagging the dog." In their increasing efforts to meet budget requirements, science centers can lose sight of the social impact they were created to have, thereby limiting their capacity to fundraise effectively.

Like many comparable institutions, TELUS Spark is challenged to quantify and articulate its social impact. Its strategic planning initiative is intent on identifying specific target audience segments and then applying appropriate metrics to measure positive outcomes. The next step is to articulate their value and to communicate that to appropriate funding partners cultivated through the process. By making clear its role and value to enhancing science literacy and contributing to a "science-ready" workforce, TELUS Spark will be in a more competitive funding position. For TELUS Spark, the strategic planning process is an opportunity to reassess the institution's revenue mix and to realign its operating priorities with its intended impacts and concomitant fundraising potential.

Benefit to the Community

The ultimate beneficiary of TELUS Spark's strategic planning process is the community it serves. Enhanced self-awareness, a better understanding of community needs and how best to meet them, engagement with prospective collaborators, and clear articulation of the organization's intended impacts and value produce a better civic partner and more rounded educational and social offerings that benefit everyone, even those who may not directly participate.

Figure 3.7 Children arriving at TELUS Spark, the new science center dedicated to twenty-first-century skills development through inquiry-based and design-thinking learning. *Courtesy of TELUS Spark.*

Chapter 4

How

Methods of Engagement

To harness the creative energy of the staff, to inspire loyalty from stakeholders and funders, and to fulfill the needs and expectations of people they are serving or wish to serve, cultural organizations need to engage with those groups of people. Strategic planning provides many platforms for such engagement. However, the planning process may be intimidating or unsettling for some of the participants. Even the words "strategic planning" can be off-putting. If people feel they have been left out, they may thwart implementation of the plan.

Principles of Strategic Planning

By adopting the five core principles of confidentiality, integrity, accountability, a 360-degree perspective, and alignment, planners can alleviate some of that anxiety, encourage greater and more enthusiastic participation, and establish a thorough, well-balanced, and efficient engagement process that will produce a realistic and workable plan.

Confidentiality

Confidentiality is key to collecting candid assessments of the institution from board members, staff, volunteers, and community leaders. People need to be reassured that their responses will be kept in strict confidence and that they will not be punished for views that may seem contrary or negative. The final report will certainly include direct quotes, but they should not be attributed to particular participants.

Board members, for example, may not want to disagree with a position they think their director holds dear, or they may not want to be perceived as "troublemakers." They will often withhold contrary opinions in the boardroom but will say what they really think in one-on-one conversations as long as they are assured that their comments will not be attributed to them.

Staff members are often even more wary of voicing opinions they think are in opposition to management's perspective for fear of retribution on the job. This is a good reason to have outside consultants conduct staff discussions and to avoid having senior management participate in workshops. Professional colleagues will not want to appear critical of an esteemed institution or peer, especially if they think the comments could be picked up by the press. Community leaders understand the weight their comments may have and may be reluctant to speak, especially if they are not experts in the field or think they may be quoted by name later.

One way of gaining candid responses from these critical segments of the community is to interview board members, professional colleagues, community leaders, and volunteers in their own settings—whether homes or offices. Given strict confidentiality and a comfortable setting, people will be completely candid in their responses. This is equally true for scheduled telephone interviews, which are often preferred by trustees and community leaders, given their busy schedules. It is much more difficult to achieve candor if you ask respondents to be interviewed within the walls of the institution.

Confidentiality may be assured by using a consultant, an unbiased "third party," to conduct the interviews or by collecting data electronically through a survey instrument tabulated by an outside party. But it is important that confidentiality be promised and kept from the beginning and be continued throughout the planning process.

Integrity

Nonprofit cultural organizations are grounded in the public trust, which is the basis for their tax-exempt status in the United States and for government support in many places. Integrity in the planning process is critical to maintaining that trust. It also means confidences will be kept, conclusions will derive from the data, interactions with the community will be transparent, and the planning process will be effective and efficient.

Very often, it is challenging to engage people in discussing an organization's options and future. The issues can be complicated and difficult. Staff members may need to get things off their chests before real dialogue can happen. Community members may not have had good experiences with the institution in the past and may not trust that things will be different in the future. Board members may be divided into enclaves.

A process based on integrity, the value of all the participants, an agreement to recognize the value of ideas, and transparency will encourage everyone to care about making the institution better.

Accountability

Another aspect of a thorough and efficient planning process is accountability. This means that those responsible are required to account for their actions. There is a clearly demarcated process available for inspection, where the reasons for decisions are clearly explained. Most cultural organizations are held in the public trust. Whether they receive public funds or, as in the United States, receive favorable tax status, they are legally responsible to the public. Accountability is necessary throughout the life of the organization, in both its annual report and its various other reports to donors and members.

There is no more important time for accountability than during the strategic planning process, when the stakes are higher than in the normal course of business.

"Deliverables" in each section of the plan should be assigned to a particular person. This clearly delineates who is accountable and is a powerful motivator in accomplishing goals.

Accountability is important to keep the organization's board, staff, volunteers, and community in alignment. It is the process by which all parties understand how decisions are made and perceive their part in the whole. The organization needs to be accountable to its community; leadership needs to be accountable to the full board. When stakeholders feel that the organization and its leadership have been fully accountable, they are much more likely to support its decisions and strategic directions.

Accountability also means that leadership is willing to be questioned and will be patient (not defensive or strident) in its responses. Leaders should be the first to speak rather than being "found out" by board, volunteers, staff, or the press. This takes maturity, integrity, respect for the opinions of others, and a good measure of self-esteem.

The strategic planning process can create tension and stress because it may change long-held ways of operating. Accountability flows from transparency and reassures all participants that any changes are the result of careful and serious deliberation, keeping the needs of the audience and the community clearly in focus.

360-Degree Perspective

For the organization to prosper, it must respond to community needs. Planners need a variety of inputs to understand how the institution functions within many different segments of its market and how it might function more effectively.

The 360-degree perspective is based on the commitment that each perspective matters and each strengthens the final result. The plan has a much better chance of success if all views are welcomed and taken into account. The 360-degree perspective is helpful in gaining buy-in from the various stakeholders and may lay the groundwork for funding initiatives resulting from planning discussions. Getting responses from the whole spectrum of stakeholders depends first on confidentiality and the integrity of the process, and it is much more likely to be achieved if the leadership is accountable to the community.

Staff at all levels have valuable insights to share. Very often, frontline staff such as security officers and front-of-house staff are more aware of audience experiences and perceptions of the organization than the most seasoned senior staff. Their observations are intensely valuable to the process and should be encouraged and included. Volunteers who work with the public, such as ushers and docents, also know well what the public responds to and how the organization is seen. Board members hear about the institution throughout the community and may have valuable insights into the perceptions of potential donors. Colleagues may have an understanding of the strengths and weaknesses of an institution that is totally different from that of its leadership. Neighbors—even those who never come inside—have opinions of the cultural organization based on facts, such as how the grounds are maintained, hearsay, and even rumors. Cultural organizations are place-makers and anchors of community life. All of these perspectives ensure that the organization will learn much more about itself during the planning process, as long as it is receptive to the information.

Sometimes it is difficult for the leadership to hear criticism, but it is important not to be hurt by comments from confidential interviews or SWOT responses. People by nature have more to say about the weaknesses of an organization than its strengths or opportunities, and they often characterize those weaknesses less delicately when the responses are anonymous. It is important to draw out any underlying issues in the ensuing discussions and to encourage people to reveal where they think the institution should concentrate its energy. The resulting internal discussions can build understanding across many kinds of divisions and can also demonstrate how hard the leadership is working at coping with complicated and difficult issues.

Alignment

Alignment is one of the outcomes to be achieved from the strategic planning process. When an institution is "in alignment," all the staff are working together to achieve the mission and all agree with the goals and objectives to deliver that mission to the public. The more closely an institution is in alignment, the more focused its collective energy can be, with all moving in the direction of the mission. To achieve this alignment, the strategic planning process needs to embrace interdepartmental and cross-disciplinary ways of working. That is why alignment needs to be a principle of the process—so that, for example, experts in one area (such as fundraising) can comment on another area (such as programming), and vice versa. Typically, different departments in the organization have very different notions about how to achieve the mission: curatorial departments may want to serve a primarily professional audience while education departments may want to serve inner-city schoolchildren. The planning process serves to increase alignment by opening up and sustaining channels of communication.

Internal Assessment

Cultural organizations collect data that should be assembled at the outset of the planning process. If key data sets, like patron demographics, are missing, there is still time to acquire that data. The organization will likely have records of revenue, attendance, ticket sales per show, salaries of full-time staff and contracts with part-time staff, membership, shop sales, geographic distribution of school tour participants, and so forth; it may also routinely survey audiences and participants in educational programs. Five- and ten-year trend lines in financial and attendance data may be quite revealing, and the organization may already have a lot of feedback in its existing data.

At institutions where the executive team gathers regularly to review the numbers, troubleshoot, and discuss broad issues, there will be solid historical data about attendance (both revenue and ticket sales), contributions, membership levels, store revenues, and the like, revealing trends in visitors, correlations between the number of visitors and the number of members, and other useful information. The director of finance formats the data contributed by the other divisions. The institution can clearly see where it has been, what has worked, what seasons are best for visitors, and what kinds of programs the community has responded to.

Other surveys may have assessed what patrons have learned, what they enjoyed most, and the level of satisfaction with their experience. Any and all data need to be brought together and analyzed to understand the institution's current situation as accurately and objectively as possible. Sometimes an outsider can look at data that management thinks it knows well and see something new or put the data in a larger context that reveals new possibilities.

In the largest sense, the stakeholders of an organization are those people who have any investment in the institution or any relationship with it, whether personal or professional. The internal assessment takes into consideration the perspectives of those closest to the organization's operations: staff, board, volunteers, donors, and members. All of these constituencies "own" the institution in some way and usually have strong feelings about the direction they want to see it follow. They spend the most time and may have invested the most money in the institution, so their opinions matter. They often have long histories with the organization and much good information to share.

It is important to create a process that includes as many members of the organization's family as possible to capitalize on their wisdom and to add energy to the implementation of the plan once it has been defined. The buy-in of all these important groups can energize an institution, just as the lack of it can stall the most carefully crafted plan. Spending more time on these constituencies in the beginning of the process can make implementation much easier. If people feel their voices have been heard and they have participated in discussions, then they are much more likely to understand why certain directions have been chosen and to be supportive in their actions and contributions.

There are a number of ways to organize internal assessment and they are discussed in the following sections.

Involving the Board of Trustees or Governing Body

Governance of not-for-profit cultural institutions differs by type of organization and is in a process of change. Libraries, for instance, are generally governed by larger organizations such as city councils or universities. Libraries will often have a separate foundation that is independent of the larger organization and raises funds for it—perhaps even organizing special events. While collecting institutions such as museums and botanic gardens are found in the government sector, more and more are becoming semi-independent government agencies or fully independent nonprofits, known as 501(c)(3) nonprofit institutions in the United States and independent charities in Canada and England. The twenty largest Italian museums are currently moving from the government to a more independent status. Performing arts organizations may also be found in the governmental and independent nonprofit sectors. Finally, many cultural organizations are being operated as public/private entities with the government and nonprofits, such as "conservancies," cooperating. All this is to say that the simple advice to involve the board of trustees in the planning process covers a great deal of complexity. In structuring the strategic planning process, a great deal of care needs to be taken to appropriately involve the governing body or bodies.

Ideally, every member of the governing body is interviewed, using the same set of questions, to learn their thoughts about the state of the organization, its threats, and its opportunities. This ensures that everyone feels part of the process, and it provides the opportunity to deepen or, if necessary, to repair relationships. Many of these interviews may be conducted more feasibly by telephone.

If the board is large and personal interviews are not feasible, board members may be involved through a series of facilitated meetings that create a dialogue. A skilled meeting facilitator is crucial, as it is important to keep as many options as possible open at the beginning stages of the process and to avoid having the group jump to any final conclusions at the outset. A designated notetaker can capture ideas; this person should not be an active participant in the conversation.

In these meetings, staff members and the director should not dominate; if possible, they should simply observe and not speak at all. If the director speaks, participants may believe that he or she has the "answer" to the issue at hand, so the discussion will be curtailed. Staying on the sidelines can be difficult, both for new directors who are still learning their roles and who may feel the need to establish credibility and for long-time leaders who are used to resolving well-known conflicts.

Engaging Staff

Staff members may also participate in group meetings facilitated by trained consultants or by staff members themselves. This can be an opportunity for cross-divisional interaction and build-ing an understanding of issues from different parts of the community. Such meetings are also opportunities for staff to develop leadership and communications skills.

At one museum, cross-divisional staff meetings, with a maximum number of participants for each meeting, were scheduled, and staff members were encouraged to attend, preferably not in departmental groups. As a result, people heard, often for the first time, the perspective of other divisions in the museum. Photo services staff made some of the most insightful comments about the work of the museum in the community; curators were intensely interested about drawing new audiences to see works of art; security staff had insights into the reasons people were attracted to certain exhibitions and not to others. The discussions were passionate. Staff came away with a new understanding and respect for others whom they might have seen in the cafeteria but to whom they had never spoken. This is often an issue in large institutions where staff may not know people who do not work closely with them on a daily basis, but even in midsized institutions a cross-divisional meeting on a specific topic will bring new understandings of a problem or issue and will help build institutional alignment.

It may also be helpful to have additional meetings with departments, so staff who deal with par-ticular facets of the institution have an opportunity to talk to their colleagues about the direction their department may take over a five-year period. This can be a marvelous opportunity for staff to "lift their heads" from their daily work and look to the future. The environmental scan docu-ment is a useful tool for this process.

Brainstorming and sharing ideas can create much excitement and reenergize people. Junior members of departments can join in the larger philosophical discussion, and their views will re-flect the younger generation's take on technology, learning styles, visitor patterns, and subjects of interest.

At one performing arts center, management and volunteers were trained in facilitation tech-niques for the staff SWOT discussions. One person led the session while another took notes on large sheets of paper so the whole group could see what was being recorded. Staff members knew in advance who was leading each session; if they did not want to speak in front of their own manager, they could choose a different session. The experience allowed managers to hear directly what staff members were thinking and to learn how to listen without directing the con-versation or the outcome. The SWOT responses included a weakness (communication) that was essentially a criticism of senior leadership. That the managers were willing to listen patiently and record honestly this response enhanced staff buy-in of the process and helped create an improved culture of open dialogue.

Techniques for Group Facilitators

You are a listener, not a leader.

The "scribe" needs to write down notes exactly as they are said. If in doubt, ask, "Have I got this right?" to be sure you are capturing exactly what the speaker intended.

People need to feel that their words and their thoughts are being transmitted and recorded.

Seek to understand, not to persuade.

Listen carefully.

Ask if anyone else wants to add or respond to the thought.

Discover if there is consensus. Dissension is fine.

Do not try to resolve the conflicts.

Pick the most important things, those that will drive you. Find the 20 percent of ideas that will provide you an 80 percent gain in investment.

For each category, come out with seven or fewer ideas. Division directors will winnow them down to three in each category.

Try to recast the raw data by placing them under major topics—you will be adding information by finding the pattern, the larger topic area.

All of the information will be sent out ahead of time so that groups can underline or check areas they think are most important.

Figure 4.1 illustrates the main results of the staff SWOT analysis.

4.2.3 Using Technology

Another way to include many "insiders" in the assessment is to create an electronic SWOT process using either the institution's information technology (IT) department or an outside service

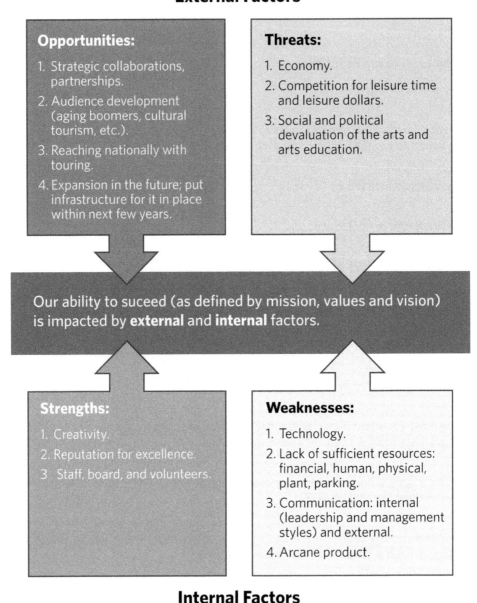

External Factors

Opportunities:

1. Strategic collaborations, partnerships.
2. Audience development (aging boomers, cultural tourism, etc.).
3. Reaching nationally with touring.
4. Expansion in the future; put infrastructure for it in place within next few years.

Threats:

1. Economy.
2. Competition for leisure time and leisure dollars.
3. Social and political devaluation of the arts and arts education.

Our ability to suceed (as defined by mission, values and vision) is impacted by **external** and **internal** factors.

Strengths:

1. Creativity.
2. Reputation for excellence.
3. Staff, board, and volunteers.

Weaknesses:

1. Technology.
2. Lack of sufficient resources: financial, human, physical, plant, parking.
3. Communication: internal (leadership and management styles) and external.
4. Arcane product.

Internal Factors

Figure 4.1 Summary of staff SWOT workshop. *Courtesy of Lord Cultural Resources.*

like SurveyMonkey to collect the data. Setting up a matrix with color codes for the different constituencies allows a very general understanding of where issues fall: if staff responses are coded blue, board members' green, and volunteers' red, it is easy to see, for example, that "technology" is a staff concern while "reaching out to new audiences" is highest on the board's mind. Comments should also be given a priority rating from one to five.

While implementing such a "high tech" methodology, it is important to maintain "high touch." One of the leaders of the planning process should make a personal appeal to the various constituencies—for example, at a meeting of the institution's volunteers or an all-staff meeting—to complete the SWOT analysis survey form. The process, as well as how the data will be used and why information from this particular constituency is important, should be explained in detail. There should be ample time for questions and answers.

In addition to the personal appeal, other methods of seeking input should be used. The organization could send out an e-mail request to its constituents with a direct link to the SurveyMonkey website or with the SWOT document attached so that responding requires only one or two mouse clicks. Communicate directly, reinforce the message in other formats (such as the members' magazine or on-site in the lobby), make responding as easy as possible, and use every opportunity to encourage participation.

Not all of the information that comes from a broad outreach SWOT analysis will find its way into the strategic plan. Often, line staff, patrons, or volunteers will make suggestions for improvements that can be taken up quickly. This can improve morale and create momentum for the larger plan. In any case, the detailed SWOT documents should be kept after the process of winnowing the ideas so that those operational concerns and suggestions can be addressed. Keep the documents on a shared drive so that everyone can see the results and participate in the full process of developing the final plan. This transparency builds understanding of both the process and the final result.

In one library, over 40 percent of the staff responded. Segments of the staff, such as security and maintenance staff, did not have individual computers. In those cases, a computer was placed in the break room and staff members were given time to use it. Staff members who were less comfortable using the computer were assisted by IT staff, who recorded their written, anonymous responses. Frontline staff members often have the most direct contact with museum visitors and have important information to share. They know how people react to services, what they think of the café, and how easy it is for visitors to find what they are looking for. Their feedback is critical and needs to be included in the current situation analysis, even if additional steps are needed to seek their views.

How Did the SWOT Process Work?

Four documents were set up electronically:

Internal Strengths Analysis (name and describe; list actions recommended)

Internal Weaknesses Analysis (name and describe; list actions recommended)

External Opportunities Analysis (name and describe; list actions to take advantage of)

External Threats Analysis (name and describe; list actions to counter or defend against)

External Assessment

For a 360-degree organizational assessment, it is important to know what people outside your institution, such as opinion leaders, community leaders, visitors, nonvisitors, peers, and experts, think of it.

Opinion Leaders

Which external voices should be included? Board members and staff leadership will be able to identify important opinion leaders in the community—that handful of people whose opinions are sought and valued by many others. Opinion leaders do not always have formal leadership roles, but they may. The specific governance structure of the organization may indicate particularly important leaders, such as the mayor of the city or the university president. Others may or may not be closely aligned with the organization, but they have an understanding of its place in the life of the community and how that could improve with a change in strategic direction. It is often useful to interview a number of people, asking for their suggestions about opinion leaders, to see which names come up again and again. Those are the top people to interview.

At one art museum, the steering committee sought opinions from a very broad group of community leaders. The museum had been thought of as somewhat remote—free to the public but not welcoming. The strategic planning process was an opportunity to engage actively with the community, to invite dialogue and suggestions. Over one hundred leaders in the community were interviewed, giving a very full picture of the museum's situation and revealing that while it was held in very high esteem, there were many avenues for improvement. At the same time, the process signaled a change in the way the institution engaged with its community—less the beaux-arts edifice on the lagoon and more the active partner, willing to listen and learn.

Community leaders have the respect of segments of the community defined in various ways: ethnicity (leaders in the Latino or Korean American community, for example); expertise (leaders in education, as in college presidents or the heads of the school board, or business, as in the head of the local chamber of commerce); elected office (city council president, for example); social network (volunteer groups and community activists in areas like the environment and housing); or geography (heads of county councils).

If the community is large and the organization wants to expand its base of contacts, it may be useful to network in advance of the planning process to identify additional community leaders who may not be close to or well known by the institution's leaders. One cultural organization invited community leaders it already knew to identify an additional diverse group of community activists—church leaders, school principals, heads of volunteer groups, and the like—to have breakfast and an hour's discussion with the director. He talked about the organization's mission of service to the community and then asked for ideas and suggestions about how he and his staff could better engage with the people whom his guests represented. It took some time to build trust with groups with whom this wealthy institution had never made overt contact, but, with perseverance and patience, the museum made friends. By the end of the process, the organization had a much fuller understanding of how it was perceived and what would help bring the community to its doors. It was also clear who among these leaders was most in touch with the pulse of the community, most articulate, and most willing to engage in the planning process to effect change.

Discussion Points for Interviews with Opinion Leaders and Community Groups

These interviews are discussions, not surveys. It is important to ask a few broad questions that will provide strategic direction. Because the resulting feedback will not be attributed to individuals, it is useful to report the results under a small number of broad categories. The following four questions produce useful answers and open up more specific issues, such as the impact of a building project or new program, if needed:

1. What is your perception of this institution?

2. What are its main challenges?

3. What are the issues, needs, and developments facing your organization (or your sector) at this time?

4. How could our institution be relevant to you, your organization, or your sector in addressing these challenges?

The consultant should interview opinion and community leaders confidentially and should report the results either by category of person (this can only be done if a large number are interviewed) or by topic. The best results require candid responses from a range of thoughtful, informed people.

Another way to involve community leaders is through workshops of five to twelve people, which add even more voices to the mix. A consultant leads the discussion and encourages all to participate while a notetaker captures the main ideas. This works especially well when there is a cross-section of people with different perspectives and when the consultant is careful not to let any one person dominate the exchange.

Communicating the Findings of the External Assessment

Communicating the findings of this important stage requires skill. What has been received are opinions and perceptions—not necessarily facts. Some perceptions will be based on events in the distant past and may be demonstrably "untrue" today. However, these perceptions demonstrate that the aura around negative events lasts a very long time—and may prevent people from engaging with an organization. For example, negative press over the treatment of animals at a zoo alienates the public long after the behavior has been corrected. Some perceptions and opinions will be highly individualized, the thoughts of a tiny minority. How does one report accurately about such perceptions without creating the misleading impression that "everyone" thinks this way, an impression reinforced when it is printed in a report? On the other hand, there will be observations that recur in many sources, often amounting to a broadly held (though rarely universal) perception. What is the best way to communicate this finding?

Choosing a method to communicate findings is a central concern in strategic planning. One approach is to provide transcripts of everything after removing names. This is costly to produce, may inhibit the sharing of forthright opinions, and takes an enormous amount of time to read. Another approach is to provide a bulleted summary, such as five learnings from each category. This leaves out the "texture" of opinion, which can only be gained from direct observation, direct quotations, or accurate paraphrases. The most effective approach is for the consultant or facilitator to summarize the findings in a sentence or two, followed by quotes and paraphrases of what interviewees actually said, placing the most frequent comments at the top of the list and the least frequent at the end. These summaries can be organized by the category of informant and by question or topic.

Even this will be too much for many board and staff members to read. This is why the steering committee discussion is extremely important, as all members of the steering committee will enthusiastically read and debate the external assessment report. Through discussion with the steering committee, the consultant or facilitator will be able to prepare the pared-down bullet-point summary for circulation to the board and staff, with the original report available upon request or as an appendix.

Visitors and Patrons

There are now a number of different methods to get responses from visitors. One way is to survey them on-site, using professionals or volunteers who have been trained in research methods. These responses will yield information from frequent as well as infrequent visitors, whose perceptions of the institution may vary widely.

It is most useful to survey regularly, using the same instrument, through different seasons or cycles of the organization's activity. This provides trend data and puts each set of survey results in the context of the history of results.

Volunteers can be trained to collect the data. They must maintain a strict discipline of intercepting every nth visitor and must not choose or avoid particular people or types of people, which would invalidate the results.

Another way to generate information is to install a computer kiosk where patrons can fill out a survey. Such surveys should ask for general demographic information in order to correlate the responses. For example, kiosk users may tend to skew younger than in-person intercepts, and that should be understood when interpreting the data. The great advantage of the computer kiosk is that the data is already in an electronic form and can be analyzed directly, without the further step of entering the information into a database.

To entice people to respond to surveys, whether in-person or at a kiosk, organizations may offer a token reward—for example, free passes for a return visit, a beverage at the café, or a discount at the shop.

Nonvisitors and Nonattenders

Professionals are generally used to obtain information from people who do not visit—in the past this has usually been done via telephone surveys. Often survey participants will not be told who is sponsoring the research. Selection of informants is important for a statistically correct sample, and this is usually best left to professionals. As a result, collecting information from nonvisitors can be costly, and, unfortunately, institutions often forgo this piece of the 360-degree view. However, there are now less expensive ways to research nonvisitors.

Why people choose not to visit is critical information. There may be widely held misperceptions that can be addressed or there may be fundamental issues that an institution needs to rectify in order to reach a wider audience.

An organization may wish to conduct focus groups to get information from nonvisitors and nonattenders. Focus groups are less costly than large telephone surveys, although professionals must conduct them. In addition, staff and board members can see and hear reactions to the institution's offerings and policies from real people in real time. The results can be quite startling and tend to make a strong impression. Focus groups conducted by one museum to gauge interest in upcoming exhibition projects revealed how much awareness building would be necessary to bring people in. That handful of "real people" talking about the museum in total candor taught the director, curators, marketing and development staff, and several board members a valuable lesson. Now, even a few years later, the people who saw the focus group in action bring up the lessons learned in discussions.

There are a number of foundations and charitable trusts that may help organizations do this critical research. One of the leaders in this field in the United States has been the Wallace Foundation, and others such as the Pew Charitable Trusts and the Bush Foundation have also supported market research. Local community foundations and individuals also help nonprofits build their infrastructure and respond to articulated community needs. Discussions at the board level about the importance of the research will communicate its urgency and can surface individuals willing to help, either by supporting it personally or asking others.

There are now also ways to use online surveys, which are much more cost effective than telephone surveys and are more likely to generate qualified respondents, since so many people no longer have landline telephones.

Peers and Experts

The 360-degree view also incorporates the perspectives of the peers (local, national, or international) and experts in the field. There are varying levels of participation possible from these very useful sources.

Local experts—colleagues from peer institutions or university professors in related fields, for example—are relatively easily identified by board and senior staff members and should be interviewed in the early stages of the process. They have the advantage not only of knowing the sector but of understanding the local environment, its opportunities, and its particular challenges. Having their names on the list of participants lends credibility to both the process and the resulting document. They should be treated with care by making appointments for the interviews (either by telephone or in person) and allowing enough time for thoughtful conversations. Be aware of any past history or biases that the individual might bring to the discussion.

Nationally and internationally known experts can bring a special excitement and fresh perspective to the process. Consultants with deep knowledge of the issues facing an institution can bring the perspective of others who have dealt with the same challenges. They may have conducted studies that help the institution make better-informed decisions. It is worth seeking the additional funding that may be necessary to support their visits to the institution. Individuals close to the institution who are interested in the expert's field may be willing to help defray costs.

Experts may be drawn from the field or from outside areas identified as critical to the organization's future (such as technology or marketing). Senior staff members can help identify experts in the field through presentations made at conferences and publications. Double-check to be sure that potential speakers are good communicators if no one has heard them give a presentation.

Institutions looking to "think outside the box" may want to consider experts from outside the sector. Such experts bring a different perspective to tough old problems (attracting new audiences, for example) or difficult new challenges (how to use technology effectively, for example).

Once outside experts have been chosen, the organization should involve as many people in interactions with them as possible. There are a number of opportunities:

- meetings with the strategic planning committee

- discussions with staff groups

- public lectures, with question-and-answer sessions, simulcast on public radio or on the institution's website

- private dinners with potential donors

A high-profile expert can also bring attention to the strategic planning process, which can be especially helpful for an institution that is seeking a higher profile. This attention creates an expectation that the resulting plan and the organization's conduct will be responsive to community needs and wishes.

Staff members are often energized through the strategic planning process, especially when it includes the opportunity to interact with famous experts. As part of its strategic planning process, the Cleveland Museum of Art invited Derrick de Kerckhove, then director of the McLuhan Program in Culture and Technology at the University of Toronto; Paul DiMaggio, professor of sociology at Princeton University; and Mihaly Csikszentmihalyi, professor of psychology at the University of Chicago—three famous experts in technology, sociology, and creativity, respectively—to visit the museum over the course of the strategic planning discussions. They had time to talk about ideas with midlevel managers in a seminar-like setting. The "not business as usual" aspect of the personal interaction, as well as the high level of the discussion, thrilled the staff.

Board members also had special access to these experts at group meetings and dinners hosted by individual trustees. This opportunity for personal communication, a stimulating educational environment, and social interaction made these meetings high points of the process for many of the board participants. The entire community also had access to the strategic planning process because the experts' public lectures were simulcast on the local public radio station, WCPN. All of these levels of interaction, branded as "Director's Forums," reinforced that the museum was open to new ideas and initiatives.

By creating opportunities for board and staff members from different parts of an organization to discuss large issues together, the leadership can improve morale, understanding, and teamwork across and throughout the institution.

The very best outcomes of visits from outside experts are the new ideas and energy that come into the plan.

Case Study 4.1

Why Strategic Planning for Cultural Organizations Needs to Include the City

Dov Goldstein

Cultural institutions are essential to the quality of urban life. What is a city without its parks, museums, theaters, and festivals? As cities grow and densify, there is greater need for public space and greater need for cultural institutions that bring people together for enjoyment and enlightenment. Cities depend on their cultural institutions to stimulate tourism, create safe places, and promote economic development. Most cities are no longer able to make major sustaining financial contributions to cultural institutions (with the exception of libraries, which are usually city agencies). As a result, cultural institutions often "forget" just how important they are to cities—and how important cities are to them. Cities develop cultural plans, control zoning and parking, impose taxes, and have influence over developers and others who can invest in culture, and they direct permitting processes that can benefit cultural institutions—or not. Therefore, when a cultural institution undertakes a strategic plan, it needs to engage with the city—including elected officials, planners, and other city staff from housing to parks and police.

Cities are growing. Over half of the world's population—54 percent—live in urban areas. And, according to the United Nations, the urban population is expected to increase to 66 percent by the year 2050. In many developed countries, 90 percent of the people live in cities. Rapidly growing cities face huge challenges: affordable housing, migration, public safety, employment, poverty, infrastructure, transportation, energy, environment, education, and health, to name a few.

Cities are increasingly working together to solve these problems and to exercise influence nationally and internationally. This is the rising "soft power" of cities, the capacity to exercise influence through culture, persuasion, and agenda setting—not through military or economic force, which cities do not have.[1] Strategic planning is the perfect opportunity for a cultural organization to find out the city's top priorities and how it can respond to them. This means conducting interviews with the mayor and elected officials, and inviting city staff to attend public engagement meetings and workshops.

For example, if the city's goal is to attract a major world event, supporting that endeavor could be a goal of the arts council's strategic plan. The arts council board includes many opinion leaders whose support the city needs, and participation in bidding for a big event can move the arts council from the margin toward the center of influence. Most cities designate "priority neighborhoods" where people are underserved and poverty may be high.

Through the strategic planning interview process, a theater company may learn that it can form a partnership with the city to provide youth training in theater to that community. The city cannot pay, but it could provide facilities and staff support. The theater company, for its part, can raise philanthropic dollars to pay the cash expenses. This positive relationship could also lead to resolving some zoning issues the theater has with the outdoor café at its downtown site.

Cities are concerned with being livable and sustainable. Creating communities that enhance both quality of life and quality of place is core to the promotion of human well-being. To that end, local, regional, and national governments have adopted the principle of cultural vitality as one of the four key pillars of community sustainability, together with social equity, economic health, and environmental responsibility. This four-pillared approach to sustainable communities recognizes that arts, culture, and heritage nurture individual and community identity, promote social cohesion, and contribute to sense of place.

A city's cultural vitality is the sum of many parts. Its expression is that of the iconic and established institutions—the *expected*—but also, increasingly with the force of urbanization, the voice of the *unexpected*, the art and culture emerging on city streets, in forgotten lanes, under dilapidated viaducts, and in reclaimed urban neighborhoods of long-empty warehouses. Because most *unexpected* culture occurs on city property, engagement between those who deliver these cultural offerings and the city is critical.

Recognizing that culture is key to sustaining healthy and vibrant urban communities, how do our cultural institutions respond and effect change? Moreover, how can these institutions engage with the cities themselves for their own strategic planning purposes?

Nearly every large, medium, and small urban community in North America has created a cultural infrastructure, typically consisting of, at the least, a social or natural history museum, an art museum or gallery, and a performing arts center. Older, established urban centers have much more. Even cities with populations under 100,000, such as Santa Barbara, California, boast this trio of institutions.

This cultural infrastructure and the institutions that embody it, as described above, are *expected* culture. Residents and visitors expect this infrastructure, and these traditional and ubiquitous cultural institutions are essential for a city to be competitive, to attract business and talent. Expected culture also draws tourists to a city and attracts newcomers to relocate.

Historically, these institutions did not consider inclusivity or accessibility as part of their DNA. But this is changing—particularly as cities expand with new immigrants and people of diverse backgrounds. Dramatically shifting demographics, digital connectivity, and cultural diversity have reshaped how museums and performing arts centers engage with the broader community.

Recognizing these tidal shifts, institutions cannot plan for their future in a vacuum. They cannot hold court with only their own staff or engage with stakeholders or rely solely on market data. Successful institutions work closely with municipalities to align their planning with city priorities, goals, and official plans as well as with secondary neighborhood plans. Workshops with key city staff and interviews with elected council members, managers, department heads, and even the mayor will shed light on the cultural organizations' challenges and inform their goals and direction for the future.

Interviews with a city councillor representing a neighborhood that comprises newcomers from other countries, for example, inform how a public garden develops and presents programs and exhibitions that reflect the cultures of the communities it serves. Direct engagement with a community representative from the city, such as a councillor or social service provider, lends a nuanced understanding of the needs and wants of a particular community.

Town hall meetings are also a very effective strategic planning tool for cultural institutions to engage with and galvanize a city around particular issues. Cultural institutions should work closely with municipalities to promote these meetings to their residents. One thing is certain: there are more residents than audiences for culture. By working with cities, cultural institutions can build greater community participation, which leads to a sense of inclusivity and ownership of their strategic plan.

Active audience participation and co-curation has most recently become a hallmark of many cultural experiences. These participatory experiences signal a dramatic shift in how museums are programmed in an effort to engage with local communities and create an environment of inclusivity and accessibility. With greater and more active community involvement, historical sites have become agents of social change. No longer are they solely repositories of stories and history; rather, they are forces shaping the conversation and social future of the city and beyond.

The notion of museums and cultural institutions as public and welcoming places very much aligns with city priorities and the need for people in urban communities to meet and gather. Museums recognize that the barriers—perceived or real—that separate the institution from the public need to be collapsed.

Forward-thinking cultural entities understand that dedicated public and communal spaces within and around them need to be dynamic, open, and programmed. These spaces welcome the public to share in activities, partake in events, or simply hang out. Often, these public spaces are facilitated by the city through planning incentives with private developers.

Urbanization has influenced how cultural institutions engage with audiences, creating more open and accessible experiences. Urbanization has also shaped how cultural institutions are planned and positioned within the urban context. For instance, cultural districts or cultural clusters are planned urban consortia of cultural institutions and organizations together with related cultural activities, services, and industries.

A key feature of the modern cultural district is the interdependency of each of its neighbors. Cultural institutions situated close to one another generate greater economic strength and attract more visitors than if they were out on their own. Successful cultural clusters aggregate activities and institutions into walkable, accessible places. These can be in urban downtown areas or parklike settings.

London's Knowledge Quarter, for example, encompasses some fifty entities including the British Library, the Francis Crick Institute, a cartoon museum, and a children's theater with pop-up activities and restaurants. This collective satisfies many interests, such as literature and science, and encourages exploration and curiosity, but it does not require a group to decide the focus of their day in advance.

Cultural districts or clusters are created by a combination of willing cultural institutions, organizations, and cultural producers; viable infrastructure; political will; and public and private support. However, cultural districts could not happen if it weren't for municipal support such as favorable zoning regulations, tax incentives, air rights sales, and density transfers. These tools can have much higher financial value than the subsidies of old—but they take strategic thinking and time to develop.

The densification of our cities and global urbanization have changed the way we move through our urban centers. As we rely less on the personal automobile, our journey becomes part of the experience of getting from place to place, and the single-destination trip becomes less desirable. This supports the concept of the cultural district; it also creates an entirely new cultural paradigm in which the city and all of its constituent pieces discovered along the way become a new form of cultural infrastructure.

Whereas *expected culture* includes the core cultural institutions of cities—art museum, performing arts center, and social or natural history museum—*unexpected culture* encompasses the found, abandoned, and reclaimed pieces of the city that have been appropriated for creative expression. Unexpected culture is the new cultural infrastructure of an urbanized world.

Deindustrialized urban cores, gentrification, and advances in public transportation and energy have created a legacy of abandoned power stations, derelict lanes, and dilapidated viaducts and underpasses. These and other remnants of an urbanized society have become canvases for artists, designers, musicians, and social activists. And their work is experienced by everybody, everywhere in the city. Unexpected culture epitomizes a city's sense of place. It fosters diversity, openness, and accessibility, the mainstays of cultural vitality.

As with *expected* culture, *unexpected* culture requires engagement with the city to be successful. The elements that compose *unexpected* cultural infrastructure belong, for the most part, to the city. Artists, grassroots organizations, and other cultural producers must work closely with the city—not just for licenses and other regulatory requirements, but also for partnership opportunities and in some instances guidance and mentorship.

Examples of *unexpected culture* abound in nearly every urban center around the world, from the now-famous High Line—a reclaimed, disused elevated rail spur in Lower Manhattan that has been transformed into an urban park and public space—to Rush Lane—an urban art gallery featuring mural art along an abandoned lane in downtown Toronto. The Bentway, a two-kilometer stretch of abandoned, city-owned space below an elevated expressway in Toronto is being transformed into a major urban cultural destination. Such initiatives could not have happened without the foresight, planning, and stewardship of the city together with private enterprise and socially conscious philanthropists.

Unexpected culture exists harmoniously with expected culture. They are both part of our urban fabric. As the world continues to urbanize, however, and we become more engaged with our city, *unexpected* culture may indeed become *expected*, and a new cycle of cultural change may emerge. And whichever way it emerges, collaboration and engagement with the city will always be a strategic element.

Figure 4.2 Cities and cultural organizations are working together in innovative ways that require strategic planning and engagement. The Bentway, pictured here in an artist's rendering, demonstrates such a public-private initiative that involved the city of Toronto working closely with a coalition of planners and philanthropists to create a park on disused city land under an expressway. *Photo credit: Public Work.*

Note

1. Gail Dexter Lord and Ngaire Blankenberg, *Cities, Museums, and Soft Power* (Washington, DC: Rowman & Littlefield, 2015).

Case Study 4.2

How Art League Houston Engaged Communities

Priya Sircar

Art League Houston (ALH) has occupied an important niche in the Houston arts landscape for over sixty-five years, supporting emerging and established contemporary artists and helping Houston residents to develop their artistic abilities. Over that period, the Houston community around ALH has experienced rapid growth and change. Already the most ethnically and racially diverse metropolitan area in the country, Houston has overtaken Chicago as the third-largest city in the United States. The regional population is projected to more than double in the next few years with a huge increase in residents aged sixty-five years and older. Other changes are on the horizon: the Hispanic population is on track to surpass the

Anglo population, people will live more urban lifestyles, self-employment will grow, and the population will be more accepting of multiple ethnicities and gay rights. Jobs for painters, sculptors, illustrators, and photographers are expected to grow.

ALH realized its heritage as a traditional art league and the first contemporary art organization in Texas is important but does not convey to the broader community how the organization has evolved. ALH also recognized that to further its legacy of serving the Houston arts community and the general public, it needed to adapt to the changing reality.

With the aim of planning for smart growth, ALH undertook a strategic planning process motivated by the desire to address four immediate priorities:

1. Create a three-to-five-year organizational plan.

2. Develop a cash reserve.

3. Pay off mortgage debt.

4. Renovate a secondary facility.

While three of the four priorities were operationally (and internally) focused, the priority of creating an organizational plan was so fundamental that it required a carefully considered engagement process to assess ALH internally and externally.

Why Community Engagement

At the start of the planning process, the ALH mission statement was "to cultivate awareness, appreciation, and accessibility of contemporary visual art within the community for its cultural enrichment." With three main components or functions—gallery, school, and community outreach—ALH is a highly public-focused organization. Within these areas, it offers a range of programs:

Gallery

*   exhibitions

*   artist board

*   public art

*   Texas Artist of the Year award

*   Lifetime Achievement Award

*   artist-in-residence program

School

- classes and workshops

- open studio figure drawing for adults

- figure drawing for teens

Community

- Healing Art program

- ArtBound! in-school artist residencies

- summer art camps

- summer high school studio intensive

ALH has a wide range of constituencies because of the variety of its program areas. For example, the ALH school attracts adults of varying ages but who skew older. ArtBound! serves schoolchildren through in-school teaching artist residencies, while Healing Art serves people with chronic illness, most of whom are middle aged or older. Meanwhile, recent exhibitions have attracted younger audiences. Additionally, ALH has constituencies who serve those groups, including permanent and part-time staff, contract teachers, and its board.

ALH's activities therefore involve a number of audiences who make up its "community," all of whom needed to be engaged to glean sufficient information on which to base decision making. Additionally, engagement with these community segments fosters in them a sense of ownership in future success—an essential ingredient for implementation of the eventual strategy.

How

The consultants and ALH engaged various segments of ALH's community through a range of methods:

- *Interviews with staff and board.* ALH's four permanent staff and three representative board members (out of ten) were interviewed confidentially, one-on-one.

- *Board survey.* An online survey provided confidential input during a transitional moment from a traditional art league board (nationwide, these boards historically have been homogeneous, wealthy, and female) to a board that was slightly more diverse in terms of race, gender, age, profession, socioeconomic status, and familiarity with contemporary art. Half the board was new to ALH.

- *Key stakeholder interviews.* Seven key stakeholders in the arts community, familiar with ALH in varying degrees and capacities, were interviewed. This group included leaders of other cultural organizations, an art critic journalist, an ArtBound! teacher, a Healing Art teacher, and a major Houston-area funder.

- *Constituent workshops.* Three workshops provided insights from artists (including those involved with ALH as teaching artists, artists-in-residence, or award winners), students (in ALH's classes and programs), and the general public, including a mix of those familiar and unfamiliar with ALH (such as volunteers and exhibition attendees). Workshops ranged from three to fourteen participants; the small facilitated conversations enabled rich discussion. The consultant team also used "round robin" introductions to open each workshop and break the ice among participants. Written exercises using notecards elicited further input from participants who might not feel comfortable sharing information publicly. In addition to discussing ALH's strengths, weaknesses, challenges, opportunities, participants were asked to provide other feedback: How has ALH impacted you artistically? Professionally? Personally? Please describe the most impactful experience you have observed or participated in as part of Art League Houston.

The list of stakeholders and groups was identified in collaboration between ALH and the consultant team to reflect the spectrum of ALH constituents. ALH staff organized the logistics for interviews and workshops. They recruited participants from their contact lists, scheduled the workshops and interviews, and provided space, A/V equipment, and refreshments. Meanwhile, the consultant team designed and managed the electronic survey, developed the interview questions, conducted the interviews, and designed and facilitated the workshops.

Findings and Results

The range of methods and audiences provided a robust understanding of ALH from different perspectives. External participants responded positively to ALH's history and current direction while sharing observations and suggestions regarding ALH's future role in the Houston community. Common themes emerged across internal and external stakeholders to indicate strengths and challenges.

Major strengths were community involvement, the diversity and accessibility of programming, the high quality of classes and events, the organization's long history, and the energy and dedication of the staff and teachers. In contrast, other areas needed attention, including the clarity of ALH's mission and identity, alignment between board and staff, financial stability, and brand awareness.

The internal assessment showed that staff and board differed in their understanding of ALH programs and activities. Board members perceived a rapid shift in programming toward exhibitions, while the staff perceived balanced growth across exhibitions, education, and community activities. Some closely involved board members felt ALH's shift had been driven by only a few people, without broad buy-in, while staff lamented that their efforts to engage the board more closely had not been successful. Board and staff diverged in their perception of the roles and responsibilities of each group. For example, some longtime board members who previously had been intimately involved in daily operations felt left behind by staff as they developed new offerings.

To address this disconnect *during* the planning process instead of afterward, a strategic planning workshop was designed to showcase the staff's work through a dynamic and detailed presentation regarding current activities and future interests. Board members responded during the staff presentation with literal "aha!" moments. This new understanding contributed to a greater appreciation of the staff and increased involvement by the board, especially by newer members, who attended exhibition openings in greater numbers and participated more actively on board committees than they had previously.

Participants expressed enthusiasm for attracting new audiences but perceived that some long-time supporters and teachers felt alienated and left out of decision making and appreciation activities. This finding resulted in ALH's strategy to develop new audiences and also to retain existing ones.

The engagement process with community stakeholders revealed that one of ALH's great strengths lay in creating a community around contemporary visual art. Many students come back year after year for the relationships they develop with teachers and fellow pupils. "You end up making very good friends," said one participant. Similarly, exhibition attendees valued the way artists and audiences were brought together through shows. The

Figure 4.3 Art League Houston artist Laura Napier invites participants to respond to questions by positioning themselves on a grid, thereby engaging the community in contemporary art. *Photo by Iva Kinnaird courtesy of Art League Houston.*

community-building component emerged so strongly from the various constituencies that it became not only a critical issue examined in the strategic planning workshop but also central to the new mission statement.

ALH Today

The direction emerging from this community engagement and the subsequent strategic planning discussion was so clear that ALH began implementing community recommendations before completing the plan. ALH upgraded systems, improved communications, and increased board engagement.

In particular, ALH updated its mission statement specifically to focus on the community and *how* the organization engages that community: "The mission of Art League Houston is to connect the community through diverse, dynamic, and creative experiences that bring people together to see, make, and talk about contemporary visual art."

Chapter 5

From Problems to Strategies

Thinking strategically is often described as if it were a talent, but it is really a learned behavior. The pinch point of the hourglass diagram introduced in chapter 3 contains three steps that model strategic thinking: identification of key issues, comparison and benchmarking, and defining strategic directions. These steps move the team from the perception that there are lots of opportunities and challenges to understanding the following statements:

- Some opportunities and challenges are more important than others.

- The "optimal future" for the next three to five years can be defined.

- There are initiatives that would move our entire institution toward that more successful future.

- There are new or improved ways of working that will increase the capacity of staff and board to get to that optimal future.

This chapter describes the tools to help the staff and trustee leadership move from episodic or anecdotal thinking about the present and future to strategic thinking.

Thinking Strategically

The phrase "thinking strategically" conjures up history classes about wars and battles that seem foreign to the cultural world of creativity and education. In fact, thinking strategically simply means asking questions and proposing answers in large, qualitative terms. It means resisting the temptation to get into the details, focusing instead on the major factors that will move an organization forward—not incrementally but substantively.

Example: Discussion of Attendance and Diversity

Discussion Facilitator: "The last strategic plan identified a goal of engaging diverse audiences. Visitor surveys show that the Garden increased diversity from 10 percent to 15 percent of

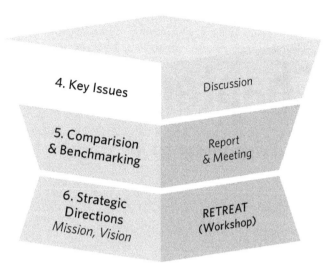

Figure 5.1 Strategic planning process: Steps, 4, 5, and 6. *Courtesy of Lord Cultural Resources.*

nonschool attendance in the last five years. Visible minorities constitute about 30 percent of the local community."

Trustee 1: "Well, when I go into the gardens, I see the same old faces. I don't think we're making much progress."

Trustee 2: "Is it really worth the marketing cost to attract these audiences?"

Facilitator: "Let's try to look at this issue in a bigger context . . ."

Trustee 3: "How are we doing relative to other cultural organizations in our community and in the country? Did we set a quantitative measure of success last time? How did we do against that?"

Trustee 4: "I wasn't on the board last time. Why did you decide that diversity was an important goal?"

The facilitator's intervention prevented the discussion from spiraling into a myriad of details. Trustees 3 and 4 responded on a more strategic level—trustee 3 pointed to the need for performance measures, and trustee 4 probed for the policy or mission basis of the goal.

Strategies are the broad approaches taken to address key issues.

There are four processes that help staff and board members make the leap from perceiving problems to developing strategies:

- identifying key issues

- comparing and benchmarking

- constructing scenarios

- discussing ideas at a strategic planning retreat or workshop

Identifying Key Issues

The findings from the research and consultations will likely result in scores of issues. The person responsible for compiling the findings should prepare a report that organizes the results by source:

- external (community) stakeholders

- staff

- nonstaff internal stakeholders

- key informants

- environmental scan

The issues can be helpfully resorted by organizational function (see chapter 1) or by theme; many themes typically emerge:

- diversity of audiences, staff, and board

- current guest experience

- physical environment

- growing collections or repertoire

- focusing programs

- new technology

- human and financial resources

- meeting community needs

Comparing the broad themes that emerge from the organization's "family" with those that emerge from the external stakeholders and those that are identified in the environmental scan can be instructive.

For the strategic planning process at the International Center of Photography in New York, the consultants and senior management summarized the internal and external inputs and reports on flip-chart sheets, which were posted on the wall to aid the steering committee in debating key issues.

Figure 5.2 Flip charts: A low-tech but essential tool in strategic planning. *Courtesy of the International Center of Photography.*

The steering committee reviews this information, discusses and debates it, and determines five to ten key issues to be taken to the retreat for further discussion and formulation of strategies.

> Key issues are like roadblocks in the way of progress. Resolving these issues using strategies will put your organization on track to be more successful.

The steering committee, composed of the board chair, the director, and selected trustees and staff, brings a comprehensive view to this challenge. However, the group may require more than one meeting to formulate the key issues list. Studying the issues may raise a need for additional information or a desire to review earlier documents. So, allow time in the process for this to occur.

Because a more integrated and less departmentally channeled approach to operations and public service would enhance most organizations in the twenty-first century, we recommend that the key issues be formulated so that they are not based solely in one department.

Take collections, for example: there may be many issues around collections: the aspiration to develop the collection, the wish to display more of it, or the desire to make the permanent collection more interesting to visitors. The facilitator should coach the committee to take a "view from five thousand feet" to formulate a key issue that touches more than one area of the museum.

So a "key issue" is not only the *need to develop our collections*. Rather, for an art museum in which the collection has grown in a reactive donor-driven way, the issue would be the *need to develop a collection strategy that links collection growth to the museum's mission*. This formulation touches on more than quantitative growth because it poses the challenge of aligning future collection growth to the museum's mission through a policy mechanism.

For an orchestra that has lost touch with the community, it would be tempting to say that *the need to perform more popular music* is a key issue. However, a statement that more strategically expresses the issue would be *the need to increase awareness of the relevance of our music programs to the community by using technology to make them accessible and by using storytelling to make them compelling*.

Strategic planning is about "moving targets"—that is why the number of key issues needs to be reduced from the scores of issues that emerge from the investigative process to five or, at the most, ten. For most cultural organizations, attendance is important. But if the organization has spent the last five years building diversity and boosting ticket sales through innovative programming, attendance may no longer be a critical area to address. The key issue may now be focused on how the theater organization affects the well-being of the entire community or how the board conducts its business in a new governance system.

By the conclusion of step 4, the strategic planning steering committee should have formulated five or six key issues to be discussed in depth by the entire board at a retreat or workshop.

However, if the steering committee decides there is insufficient information about these key issues to have a productive discussion, the experience of others can be helpful.

Comparison and Benchmarking

There are many ways of bringing an external perspective to the strategic planning process. In chapter 4, we described the benefits of inviting experts from a variety of related fields to participate in director's forums. Experts can also be invited to address staff and trustee workshops. Providing the guests with the key issues report so they can discuss their experience in a way that is relevant to your situation is the key to making these encounters strategic rather than just "interesting."

At the outset, comparison and benchmarking should be distinguished from each other. Most cultural organizations like to compare themselves to others—so much so that in the United States, England, and Canada, many cultural associations and funding authorities maintain banks of comparative data that make it relatively easy to identify peers by type, size, attendance, and budget. Your organization can contact peer organizations by e-mail or phone, or possibly visit them, to learn in depth how they address similar key issues. In this way, your organization can learn about the successes and failures of different strategies, what they cost, and their benefits and drawbacks. If, for example, your organization has identified governance as a key issue and you are considering moving from a city-owned status to a fully independent not-for-profit organization, learning how similar organizations made that transition will be very useful. This comparative analysis can be conducted by a member of the steering committee or by a consultant. The results should be presented in a concise report that will inform the steering committee and the board.

Benchmarking is a process of investigating how other organizations—including those that are not even cultural institutions and those not similar to yours—have tackled similar key issues. In benchmarking, choose another institution known for achieving excellence in an area that is critical to the issues you face. The benchmark institution could be a different size and from an entirely different sector. The analysis is focused on how excellence has been achieved and maintained in an area considered critical by the strategic planning steering committee. Areas such as visitor services, innovation, human resources, and community engagement are very appropriate for such research. Benchmarking must be conducted through site visits and face-to-face discussion because it involves studying institutions that operate on a different scale or in another discipline than the organization conducting the analysis. For example, a science center might want to learn from a library how to achieve high levels of participation through web-based technology off-site as well as on-site. Or a botanic garden might want to learn how a public television station engages people in environmental issues.

Whether you choose a comparison or benchmarking process, define the type of information you seek and prepare a research plan in advance of the interviews and visits. The report on the process should be concise and focused on the key issue the steering committee is debating.

Constructing Scenarios

Groups can more easily make decisions when they can see how the future might look if different strategies were followed. Once the key issues have been identified and agreed upon, the facilitator could develop three different scenarios to demonstrate possible futures. For example, the ABC Industrial Museum faces three key issues:

- Industry stakeholders are not interested in the museum and are not providing financial support.

- Old and outdated exhibits have led to declining public interest.

- Staff are discouraged, and there is high turnover. There have been five directors in three years.

On the other hand, the interview processes revealed some opportunities:

- The region is being repositioned as a center of innovation to attract new industries.

- The community college near the museum is growing and sees the potential to offer specialist technology training at the museum, using some of the old equipment.

- Young families are moving into the area, yet there is neither a children's museum nor a science center nearby.

- The current director is committed to stay if there is a plan with forward momentum.

The facilitator, working with the strategic planning steering committee, develops the following four scenarios:

Scenario 1: Close the museum. Recognize that the museum is failing. Dispose of the collections in a professionally correct way, mainly by making donations to other museums in the area. Sell the building to the community college to pay off any debts and the costs incurred as a result of the shutdown.

Scenario 2: Merge with the community college. Maintain a minimal museum presence that tells the history of the industry, and reduce operating costs by deemphasizing the public dimension of the museum. The community college would adapt the building for teaching and training.

Scenario 3: Reinvent the museum. Transform the ABC Industrial Museum into a science center or a children's museum.

Scenario 4: Develop the existing museum. Obtain foundation support to improve the exhibits, making them more appealing to children and families. Have an aggressive marketing strategy to regain industry support.

If the director has prepared a description of his or her vision for the future of the museum, then this could be presented as the recommended scenario.

At the strategic planning retreat, there will be a lively discussion about these scenarios. Each is an oversimplification—a caricature of the future. But scenarios—like cartoon characters—provide insight. As the discussion deepens at the retreat, new futures may emerge. For example, the retreat might recommend strategic steps to explore the feasibility of scenario 3 in combination with some elements of scenario 2.

The strategic planning committee will be in the best position to determine which of the tools discussed in this chapter will be most effective in helping the board and staff leadership make decisions about strategies and goals at the retreat.

The retreat is one of the most important tools because it provides a forum for informed discussion and genuine dialogue. The retreat is such a significant process that it merits its own chapter.

Case Study 5.1

The Role of Strategic Planning in Formalizing and Communicating the Changing Role of the Toronto Zoo

Ted Silberberg

Zoos have come a long way from their nineteenth-century origins as menageries that housed tightly caged animals taxonomically (monkey house, cat house), evolving by the latter part of the twentieth century to create spaces that match each animal's specific habitat. In the twenty-first century, zoos focus on "saving animals from extinction (SAFE)"—a slogan first developed by the Association of Zoos and Aquariums (AZA).

The Toronto Zoo was established in 1974 on a seven-hundred-acre site that is the home of five thousand animals. Owned by the city and reporting to the city council, the zoo is a great family attraction and remains the largest zoo in Canada and the one with the highest attendance. The Toronto Zoo also has the highest attendance and earned income percentage among all the not-for-profit attractions in Toronto. But for the city-appointed board and staff of the Toronto Zoo, its most important measure of success is not attendance or revenue, it is the work the zoo does to save and protect species and their habitats in Canada and around the world. As noted in the Toronto Zoo Strategic Plan 2015–2020, visitors who attend the zoo's exhibits see only part of the program. The polar bear program, for example, is not just the exhibit people love to visit; it also consists of reproductive research and scientific research in nutrition and veterinary care, a conservation-focused role the visiting public often does not know or think about.

Over the years the strategic plans of the Toronto Zoo had been management-prepared documents that sought to establish its direction for periods of five to ten years. In 2015 senior management invited outside consultants to lead a strategic planning process that was far more inclusive than those that had taken place in the past. The process included numerous workshops with board members, senior management, staff, volunteers, and representatives of existing and potential partner organizations, as well as an online survey and opportunities for staff and volunteers to provide confidential comments. After the seven goals and twenty-seven associated objectives of the strategic plan were formalized, six teams of staff worked on detailed action plans intended to lead to implementation within the five-year planning period.

When the most recent strategic plan was initiated, it was clear that most staff saw conservation impact as the most important goal of the Toronto Zoo, but most board members saw governance and capital funding issues as the primary concern. Within the strategic planning process board members changed their minds, and the focus shifted to the centrality of conservation. Data from a World Wildlife Fund report indicating that the world's population of fish, birds, mammals, amphibians, and reptiles declined overall by 52 percent between 1970 and 2010, far faster than previously thought, spurred this shift.

The focus on conservation impact was reflected in new mission, vision, and values statements and to a reordering of the goals initially contemplated by the board.

The zoo's new mission is to be "a living centre for education and science, committed to providing compelling guest experiences and inspiring passion to protect wildlife and habitats."

The vision statement was modified to emphasize the national leadership of the Toronto Zoo and its responsibility to the future: "Canada's national leader in saving wildlife to ensure the rich diversity of nature for future generations."

The new core values of the Toronto Zoo begin with collaboration:

- *Collaboration.* We conduct ourselves in a manner that fosters respect and teamwork among staff, volunteers, and our partners to achieve our mutual goals.

This statement emphasizes both internal collaboration and external partnerships that the zoo is continuing to develop with conservation-focused organizations, universities, government agencies, and others. The zoo's other values follow:

- *Integrity.* We are transparent and committed to best practices and leading by example.

- *Passion.* We are proud, energetic, and passionate about saving wildlife and will inspire others to value the critical role of our zoo.

- *Excellence.* We ensure the highest standard of care for wildlife, provide excellent guest service, and create fun and transformational experiences that connect people to nature.

- *Innovation.* We encourage creativity, strive to think differently, and turn our ideas into actions.

- *Conservation.* We are committed to practicing and promoting activities and actions that benefit wildlife and the environment.

The centrality of the mission, vision, and core values statements have been communicated to all staff members and the general public by means of plaques and other postings in public spaces, staff areas, and online.

Agreeing to the order of the seven goals was an important part of the planning process, as was wording that tied some of the goals back to conservation. The well-discussed and carefully worded goals of the Toronto Zoo for five years and beyond are as follows:

1. Conservation Impact: Advance to a zoo-based conservation center of excellence.

2. Guest Engagement: Enhance the guest experience to appeal to a more diverse audience and inspire conservation action.

Toronto's residents are increasingly diverse, and the zoo aspires to widen its appeal to all in the community to increase attendance and revenues but also to inspire more people to action in support of conservation.

3. Governance: Enhance the governance structure.

The zoo's objectives included establishing a fundraising entity independent of the city that will enhance the appeal of this city-owned zoo in the eyes of potential donors.

4. Financial Stability: Build an organization that is fiscally and environmentally sustainable for the long term.

5. Strategic Alliances: Maximize existing partnerships and identify new opportunities.

The Toronto Zoo is unique in North America as a gateway to a national urban park. Plans have already been developed for a substantial level of collaboration with the park, including the possibility of a shared education facility.

6. People: Create an organizational culture that attracts, engages, and retains highly motivated staff and volunteers.

7. Understanding and Caring: Increase awareness, understanding, and support of the zoo as a center for conservation excellence.

As the order of the seven goals indicates, everything at the Toronto Zoo begins and ends with conservation.

Staff and volunteer buy-in of the strategic plan was successful not only because of an inclusive planning process but also because of clear awareness that the plan was built on the earlier successes of the zoo. This included acknowledging that the breeding programs and reproductive research of the Toronto Zoo have revived and returned endangered species to their environments over many years. The Toronto Zoo has also pioneered nutritional, animal care, and enrichment programs, and various other programs that have helped to save species and habitats.

The strategic plan was completed in 2015 and is intended to guide the board and staff of the Toronto Zoo in its actions and decisions for the next five years and beyond. The plan is a visual and focused thirty-two-page document for the general public that has been widely distributed and is available online. It has helped the Toronto Zoo achieve reaccreditation with the Association of Zoos and Aquariums (AZA) and has provided the basis for launching a fundraising foundation. Many of the staff-developed action plans have already been implemented. A fifteen-year master plan that builds on the goals and objectives of the strategic plan has been developed. Toronto Zoo CEO John Tracogna calls the strategic plan a "living document" that has formalized and communicated the changing role of the zoo and has "broaden[ed] the support of internal and external stakeholders."

Figure 5.3 Twenty-first-century zoos have evolved from their roots in nineteenth-century menageries to become centers of conservation excellence: animal artists at the Jardin des Plantes, Paris, from *L'Illustration*, August 7, 1902 (*left*); Toronto Zoo (*right*).

Case Study 5.2

A New Governance Strategy for the Tom Thomson Art Gallery

Virginia Eichhorn

Tom Thomson (1877–1917) is Canada's iconic artist. The art gallery dedicated to his life and art, and to innovative contemporary Canadian art, is located in Owen Sound, a small northern city near where he was born and educated. Having opened in a purpose-built facility in 1967, Canada's centennial year, as an arm's-length department of the city, the gallery has charted a new path to become an independent, stand-alone, nonprofit charitable organization. This strategic direction is a result of collection growth, declining city funding, and a fuller appreciation of the opportunities for a gallery of national, historic, artistic, and emotional importance.

When the museum was founded, the city assumed all costs for its operations, including a provision for covering any deficits. Surpluses were to be turned over to the museum to use for capital or other needs. By the late 1980s the city was funding approximately 85 percent of our annual budget, but by 2015 the city's contribution had declined to about 25 percent. We had successfully created additional income from arts council operating grants and multiyear sponsorship agreements as well as earned revenue, but our status as a city department prevented us from qualifying for many funding opportunities from foundations and corporations, which will not fund municipalities. The gallery has thus been seriously limited in our ability to make up the steadily decreasing city financial support.

In 2014 the museum passed an audit that qualifies us to give tax receipts for donations of art as a Category A organization. However, the audit noted that our storage vault was at capacity. If we were not able to expand the vault or find alternative storage, then we would not be able to continue to collect. If we did continue collecting, we would lose our Category A designation because we would not be housing the collection to the standards of the designation. As director, I made the decision in 2015 to cease collecting except for those donations that were already in process. The gallery was also at capacity for programming, exhibitions, and staff, so the need for an expanded facility and a capital campaign was now critical.

The administration of the organization was equally challenged by a confusing system of reporting to multiple constituencies: as director, I reported to my board, to the city council, and to the city manager. This became especially complicated as we were negotiating the separation of the gallery from the city. The negotiations at times were difficult, and the parties involved sometimes held opposite opinions about how to move forward.

The board and staff worked together to develop a clear strategy and formulated a process to achieve incorporation as an independent organization. Unfortunately, there were exceedingly few examples of organizations that had gone through a comparable process. As no other department had separated from the city previously, this raised a wide range of community and political concerns.

In order to ensure that these concerns were addressed and that we were confident in the decisions and recommendations we were making, we added board members with business and government experience. The skill sets of the board members, coupled with professional legal services, were essential for negotiating complex issues such as the art loan and lease agreements, the by-laws, and the transfer of employees to the new entity.

The board took a strong leadership role in progressing to our new governance status, and they were committed and prepared to take calculated risks in order to achieve that goal. They developed a communication strategy to sell the need for incorporation to the city, the public, and the media. We hosted a series of public and member meetings to provide information, answer questions, assuage concerns, and garner support for both the incorporation and the expansion, which was becoming increasingly essential for our continued successful operation. Regular communiqués were issued by the board chair to the membership about where we were in the process. We sought meetings with community groups and opinion makers within the community to inform them and to generate support for our plans.

The transition committee of the board was established to steer the complex issues associated with the transition of a city department to an independent incorporated entity. The transition committee, with the board's support, commissioned an in-depth report to support and articulate our goal. A consultant with a background in legal issues who had worked extensively with public art galleries was hired to work with me and the chair of the transition committee to produce "The Case for Incorporation and Expansion." This sixty-seven-page document included extensive evaluations of comparable public art museums and their operations through which we made our case for incorporation, a five-year business plan with an estimate of the economic impact of the gallery on the community, and an evaluation of two potential sites for our expansion. This was presented at an open council meeting and at a public meeting, and it was also made available through our website. "The Case for Incorporation and Expansion" garnered widespread community support.

The city council established a committee consisting of the mayor, two city councillors, the chair of the museum board, and the chair of our transition committee; the city manager and I acted as staff for the committee. This committee met several times throughout the year to resolve the most pressing issues that stood in the way of the incorporation:

- ownership of the collection and a loan agreement

- benefit coverage for transferred employees

- governance structure for the new independent gallery

- continued financial support from the city for the gallery

- lease for the current gallery building until we could move to new premises

- property tax status

In consultation with the attorneys for both the gallery and the city, an agreement was reached. On August 8, 2016, the city manager presented a report to the city council recommending that the council approve the gallery incorporating and becoming a separate entity. The council passed the recommendation unanimously. We are now in the process of moving forward with our new vision and strategic direction.

Almost a hundred years ago, Tom Thomson wrote, "Someday they will know what I mean."[1] That spirit and sentiment inspires the Tom Thomson Art Gallery, board, foundation, volunteers, and staff—past and present.

Figure 5.4 View of *Community Curators Select IV* at the Tom Thomson Art Gallery in Owen Sound, Ontario. This fourth annual exhibition features works of art from the gallery's permanent collection selected by community curators. *Courtesy of the Tom Thompson Art Gallery.*

Note

1. Quoted in Blodwin Davies, *A Study of Tom Thomson: The Story of a Man Who Looked for Beauty and for Truth in the Wilderness* (Toronto: Discuss Press, 1935).

Chapter 6

From Strategies to Goals

The Strategic Planning Retreat

The leadership retreat or workshop is the turning point of the strategic planning process because at this event the entire board and the staff leadership set the strategic direction and goals of your cultural organization for the next three to five years. The retreat should be a stimulating and energizing experience. Most retreats are successful. Some feel successful on the day but a few days later the result, and therefore the utility of the effort, seems confused and unclear. And some retreats are disasters.

If the retreat has been well planned, it is more likely to be a success. In such cases, even if something negative happens—such as irreconcilable differences among individuals, poor facilitation, or a sudden resignation—the majority of participants will understand the value of the process and be willing to try again.

The strategic planning steering committee needs to determine several things in advance of the retreat.

1. What is the reason for the retreat? The committee should develop a brief description of why a retreat is the best format for discussing and determining the organization's future, and it should identify the objectives for the day.

2. Who is invited? All board members plus the staff on the strategic planning steering committee and staff members who are part of the senior management team should be invited. Retreats are usually intended for the working board. However, it is up to the steering committee to recommend and for the board to decide whether emeritus or honorary trustees should be invited. If there is hybrid governance, it may be that foundation members should be invited. If the organization is an advisory board to a government body, consider government representation and whether that representation would be elected officials or executive personnel. There should never be more staff members than trustees at the retreat.

3. What are the details of the retreat and how long should it last? The agenda of most strategic planning retreats can be completed in four to six hours. This means that the retreat can be conducted in one day including a congenial lunch. However, some boards may see the retreat as an opportunity for socializing and learning. They may want a two-day retreat that combines some recreational activities with a full-day agenda. Or they may want to have a dinner the prior evening with a guest speaker and spouses and partners in attendance. Other boards may choose to complete the agenda within one weekend day or one business day. They may prefer to meet locally to limit travel time. The strategic planning steering committee should prepare a survey that board members can complete to indicate their preferences with respect to duration, logistics, and any dietary or other requirements. This form should also indicate that trustees will pay their own meal expenses and other retreat costs. That way, the retreat logistics will meet the preferences and expectations of the majority of trustees.

4. When should the retreat be scheduled? The date for the retreat should be set well in advance (six months is ideal) and should be announced at a board meeting. In addition, personal letters of invitation cosigned by the board chair and the director should be sent to invitees. These letters should indicate the reason for the retreat and what preparation is expected.

5. Where should the retreat be held? It is a good idea to meet in an environment different from where board and staff meetings are usually held, even if you have excellent meeting facilities. The main criteria for a location include the following:

- convenient access

- attractive and comfortable

- well-lit with windows

- conference or U-shaped table to accommodate all participants for plenary sessions

- conferencing technology, as some trustees may need to participate by phone

- technology for presentations

- flip charts and markers

- microphones so that everyone can hear

- break-out rooms for small-group discussion and lunch (Most retreats will involve break-out sessions with up to five groups; this can be done in one large room with five round tables or in five small meeting rooms.)

- a good caterer for meals and snacks

6. Preparation: By the time of the retreat, all participants should be familiar with the strategic planning process. There should have been board discussions of the environmental scan and the findings of the various investigative processes. Many trustees will have participated in workshops or interviews. The staff leadership will have been engaged on the steering committee or will have read the various reports and participated in workshops. In advance of the retreat, participants should receive a package that includes the following:

- the previous strategic plan

- the environmental scan discussion paper

- other strategic planning reports from the current process

- the key issues paper

- the retreat agenda

Setting Realistic Objectives for the Retreat

About six weeks prior to the retreat, the strategic planning steering committee should review the progress made to that point and determine realistic objectives for the retreat. Most important is to understand which decisions can be made at the retreat and which should be made at subsequent board meetings. A retreat or workshop could achieve the following objectives:

- *informing* participants about the organization's performance and position or about management's plans and strategies

- *discussing* management's plans and key issues

- *reviewing and commenting* on foundation statements and other policies

- *articulating* a common understanding of the mission and vision

- *generating* goals for the next three to five years

- *formulating* strategies to address key issues

- *deciding* priorities

- *adopting* goals

There is a great difference between articulating and adopting, between dialogue and decision. The strategic planning committee needs to be realistic about what can be achieved. Further, the facilitator needs to be skilled in making judgments on the spot. For example, the committee may think that the board is ready to adopt goals—but at the retreat new issues may arise and trustees may want to revisit earlier steps in the process or to table the goals until more research is conducted. On the other hand, the steering committee may think those at the retreat will not want to decide on priorities, for example, because of conflict about the priorities, yet the retreat discussion may reveal a greater degree of agreement than expected. The facilitator then needs to change course by encouraging the group to make a decision.

Decisions at retreats are usually made by consensus, a form of agreement based on the result of a discussion, not a vote. The facilitator judges whether consensus has been reached by one or all of the following means:

- recording all the opinions in a transparent manner on the flip charts

- inviting each participant to briefly state his or her view

- summing up all aspects of the discussion

The facilitator then identifies whether consensus has been achieved and asks the group members whether they agree. Sometimes there is consensus with certain reservations, so the facilitator might say: "There seems to be consensus on the top three goals for the strategic plan—building attendance, expanding the collection to include natural history, and investing in digital technologies throughout all aspects of the organization. However, there seem to be reservations about whether a new building should be a goal at this time. I'd suggest that management develop a paper on the pros and cons of this goal and present it at the next board meeting so you can consider this item further."

The retreat participants are not empowered to adopt anything on behalf of the organization. Rather, their decisions are, in effect, strong recommendations to the governing body, which would adopt policies, foundation statements, and ultimately the strategic plan at a duly constituted board meeting.

The Retreat Agenda

An agenda should be sent to participants two weeks prior to the retreat. It should communicate the objectives of the day, the location, start and finish times, and the agenda items, including meal and rest breaks. This sample agenda for a one-day retreat focuses on discussing key issues, developing strategies for addressing the issues, and adopting goals. A review of the foundation statements is also planned. Clearly, the steering committee believes that the board members and staff leaders are ready to make decisions. Parts are for general distribution rather than for those who are presenting and facilitating.

ABC Strategic Planning Retreat
Community Foundation Boardroom

Location, Date

8:30   Coffee

9:00–9:30   Welcome and Introductions (led by the cochairs of the strategic planning committee)

9:30–9:45   Objectives of the Retreat (led by the facilitator, who also explains the ground rules)

- to provide information about the organization's current position

- to discuss the key issues facing ABC

- to identify strategies that address these issues

- to review the foundation statements

- to agree on three to five goals for the next five years

9:45–10:30   Key Issues (presentation by cochairs of the strategic planning committee)

10:30–11:45   Discussion in Breakout Groups

Each person's name tag has a breakout group number. The facilitator explains the charge of each group and hands out an instruction sheet to the volunteer facilitators. Each group then discusses one of the key issues and comes up with strategies to address it. A member of the group who is not part of the staff will report to the gathered participants during the working lunch.

11:45–noon   Break (Lunch set-up, buffet)

12:00–1:30   Plenary Session: Strategies Moving Forward (working lunch)

Groups report back on their discussions and conclusions at 15 minutes each, followed by half an hour of questions and answers. The facilitator wraps up with a long list of strategies.

1:30–2:30   Review of Mission, Vision, and Mandate

Facilitator encourages brainstorming about what words best express the mission and vision.

2:30–2:45   Break

2:45–3:45   The Goals of the Strategic Plan

Facilitator explains what goals are and animates a process whereby the group brainstorms goals and then prioritizes them.

3:45–4:15   Wrap Up and Next Steps
              Facilitator

4:15–4:30   Thank You and Adjournment
              ABC Director

The following agenda is for a half-day workshop with a different focus. In this organization, the director has prepared a draft strategic plan (the management plan) based on input from the internal and external assessments. The workshop participants will discuss the management plan, then discuss key issues and define strategies to address them. The strategic planning steering committee had debated when the review of the mission statement should take place on the agenda and decided to review it twice—once at the beginning of the workshop and again at the end to see if participants think changes need to be made. The main objectives of this workshop will be to provide input into the director's draft plan and the ABC mission statement.

The LMN Strategic Planning Workshop
A Corporation Boardroom, Downtown

Date

Objectives

- To inform the trustees of management's plans

- To gain consensus on main strategies going forward

- To review the mission statement

- To clarify the next steps in preparing the strategic plan

Buffet lunch at noon

Welcome and introductions (15 minutes; led by the cochair of the steering committee)

Overview of the strategic planning process to date and review of mission statement (20 min; led by facilitator)

Presentation of management plan (20 min; led by the LMN director)

Plenary discussion (30 min; led by facilitator)

Breakout groups on three key issues (45 min)

Break (15 min)

Plenary discussion on the breakout groups' recommended strategies (led by facilitator)

Prioritizing strategies (45 min; led by facilitator)

Articulation of mission statement, wrap-up, and next steps (30 min; led by facilitator)

Thank you (presented by LMN director)

Retreat Report

The retreat report is a concise document usually prepared by the facilitator using the flip charts generated during the meeting. The purpose of the report is to record the ideas that emerged and the consensus that was achieved (or the differences that were recorded) for each agenda item. The retreat report is reviewed and approved by the strategic planning steering committee before being circulated to the board and staff.

Should the retreat be recorded? There are undoubtedly circumstances when video and audio recording of a retreat can be helpful. But, in general, it is cumbersome to do and to review, and it definitely will inhibit discussion of controversial issues. For these reasons, recording the retreat is not generally recommended.

The retreat report should conclude with the list of next steps and deadlines to take the process through the remaining steps: setting departmental objectives, writing the strategic plan, presenting the plan to the board, and completing the evaluation cycle. This is another turning point in the process because the focus shifts from the board to the management and staff who will write the plan.

Case Study 6.1

Creativity Is Center Stage in Strategic Planning for Roundabout Theatre Company

Lauren A. Merkel and Julia C. Levy

In the performing arts, many argue that planning five years into the future is too lengthy a time horizon. When planning productions on Broadway, it is often difficult to know which artists may be available for the selection of plays and musicals that comprise the season or what the competition may be. And market dynamics have not been in the industry's favor: four out of five shows fail, reviews can have a disproportionate influence on sales, and technology has dramatically affected the industry through discounted ticket prices and altered consumer behavior. In addition to facing the many variables in the industry, Roundabout Theatre Company has additional challenges as a nonprofit organization competing alongside commercial theaters. In such a mercurial environment, a quick, nimble, and highly responsive nonstrategy strategy may seem more suitable than a nice and neat, if not rigid, strategic plan.

Founded in 1965 in New York City, Roundabout operates four theaters with five stages (three of which are Broadway theaters eligible for Tony Awards). It produces eight shows every year and has a national reach through its world-class education programs and show tours. The size and breadth of its footprint are large. For much of its history, Roundabout had strong ticket sales from ticket subscribers and single-ticket buyers. Earned revenue ranged from 70 percent of income to 100 percent of income during extraordinary seasons like 1997–1998, which featured *1776*, *Cabaret* (Tony award) and *A View from the Bridge* (Tony award). Needless to say, Roundabout had come a long way from its early beginnings in a Chelsea supermarket.

In the performing arts, planning is commonly led by the artistic director rather than by executive management or the board. This is very much the case at Roundabout. Todd Haimes, a visionary who has created programs way ahead of their time, has steered the ship for thirty-four years. Under his leadership and praiseworthy instincts, it has grown to become the largest nonprofit theater company in the nation. As a result, Roundabout is a shining success story, serving more than one million theatergoers each year. Recently, its reach has grown through live high-definition streaming of its productions, a first in the industry. Roundabout is guided by the following mission:

> We are committed to producing the highest quality theatre with the finest artists, sharing stories that endure, and providing accessibility to all audiences. A nonprofit company, we fulfill our mission each season through the production of classic plays and musicals; development and production of new works by established and emerging writers; educational initiatives that enrich the lives of children and adults; and a subscription model and audience outreach programs that cultivate and engage all audiences.

The Impetus for Planning

As any business or nonprofit knows, despite the best talents and truest convictions, crises do happen. For Roundabout, the story begins in 2008, as so many stories in the United States do. Enter the financial crisis, the antagonist in the form of the "Great Recession." As people began to reel in the aftermath of the crash, consumer spending declined, donations stagnated, and many organizations, including Roundabout, had to take a hard look in the mirror and see how they could survive. The crisis was so unexpected and far-reaching that it became an existential risk: If major corporations buckled in its face, how was a nonprofit theater company to withstand its force? And what of other unforeseen crises? The financial crisis proved to be a watershed moment for the company and its approach to future planning.

Almost immediately, planning began to take hold as a response to the difficult economic times and the changing market. First, the industry's financing structure was dramatically changing; disposable income dropped and people pulled away from making long-term commitments like buying yearly subscriptions. At the same time, the proliferation of discounting prices online was hurting Roundabout's single-ticket revenue and the earned revenue of the industry as a whole. And, finally, there was more product on offer on Broadway—commercial producers adopted Roundabout's long-held model of shorter runs of classic plays with stars—but the industry's pie did not grow; audience numbers did not increase.

Fortunately, Roundabout has a committed and supportive board and strong leadership that recognized the shifting dynamics. In one of the meetings of the board, a trustee spoke up and said, "We need to look at our model and we need to fix it." In one short sentence, *business as usual* was no longer suitable or acceptable. The die was cast, and work earnestly began toward revamping the company business model. A small committee of the board in collaboration with the senior management team was assembled. Outside counsel was sought, benchmarking and analyses of comparables were completed, and an operating plan was presented to the board. An internal strategic planning process ensued with many unexpected insights.

One critical finding was put front and center: Roundabout had a structural deficit. The company went from performing in a space with two theaters—that also housed the administrative offices—to operating four theaters and administrative offices in five different locations. It had lost its economy of scale in operations. Many commentators (including those at the *New York Times*) thought Roundabout had an "edifice complex," an unquenchable thirst for buying more and more property. Studio 54 was purchased first, then the opportunity for a long-term lease of the Stephen Sondheim Theatre (formerly Henry Miller's) presented itself five years later. As it turns out, Todd Haimes believed in the benefits of such theaters beyond their performance value—namely, their potential to offer much-needed rental income and the opportunity to stage productions that had much longer potential runs than a subscription run.

The strategic planning review revealed another important finding: the need to capitalize the organization so it could afford to take risks in its business and artistic decisions. Roundabout's capitalization ratios were below industry standards and those of its closest competitors. Proper capitalization would empower the company to select productions for the stage that may not have inherent audience appeal but deserve to be on stage for their creativity or as important parts of the theatrical canon. It would also allow for the development of new programs as was done with the Underground, a space for emerging artists to showcase their work, or for workforce development that serves a growing need in the field.

As part of its hard look in the mirror, Roundabout also opened its books to the board, and they all dove in. The board and senior staff looked at all operations: earned and contributed revenue, artist development initiatives, education programs, and the archives. They questioned the organization's very mission to see if it was still relevant. And then they asked themselves, "Do we need to be doing everything we are doing?" The short answer was "no," and first out the door were new musical productions. A thorough analysis of the numbers revealed that new musical productions were more expensive to stage and had a lower return on investment. The season was also reduced by one play. By equal measure, other factors were deliberately retained, such as the subscription model—a core value of Roundabout. And musical revivals, as opposed to new musicals, remain an important and unique part of Roundabout's mission—they represent five of the nine Tony Awards that Roundabout has won. Finally, the board was adamant about retaining its commitment to providing arts education, an essential aspect of the company's mission.

Roundabout has a culture of calculated risk-taking, a key factor in its success. Roundabout has not avoided those risks that shape the future of theater for the better. One such example is the Associate Artist program that grew out of a need and a problem in the New York City market. The cost of living made it prohibitively expensive, if not impossible, for many artists to stay, live, and work in New York. Thus, the Associate Artist program was aimed at directors, to say to them, "You are a part of our family and we want to be your creative home." This program is a home for artists at all stages of their careers. Notable enrollees have included Scott Ellis, Kathleen Marshall, Joe Mantello, Pat Mckenon Kinnon, and Sam Gold. The Technical Theatre Workforce initiative, the first program in the industry to create a pipeline for public school graduates to enter backstage crews, is another example of Roundabout's strategic risk-taking.

And as though to underscore the turning point that was the decision to reassess its approach to conducting business, the upcoming fiftieth anniversary of the company was to be a celebration of how far Roundabout had come and a reaffirmation of its core mission to produce the highest-quality theater for all audiences. But it was also to be a look to the future and the promise of a better world through theater, one community at a time. Roundabout at fifty was given a tribute in the most fitting of ways: stakeholders celebrated its history and impact on the community through the eyes of the audiences, artists, and staff who told stories of how Roundabout affected their lives.

The Outcome of Planning

It is often said that the process is as important, if not more important, than the outcomes—and that has been true for Roundabout. Great things can come out of strategic planning: hidden gaps can be identified, new avenues and thought processes can be developed, and inspiring and energizing ideas can be shared from all stakeholders.

Roundabout's planning process was commissioned in 2010 and resulted in the presentation of clear, actionable goals and objectives. The company learned that it needed to have a reserve fund in place, to raise more money, and to grow its board. It also moved to retire bonds on a theater it had purchased and reconsidered the benefits and challenges of producing musicals.

Figure 6.1 *Long Day's Journey into Night* was part of the fiftieth-anniversary season at Roundabout. Starring (*left to right*) John Gallagher Jr., Michael Shannon, Gabriel Byrne, and Jessica Lange (Tony award), it was performed at the American Airlines Theatre, one of Roundabout's five stages. *Photo credit: Joan Marcus.*

So while Roundabout may not consider itself an organization with a planning culture, it sees the importance of being proactive, rather than reactive. It wants to be ready for the changes it sees happening in the future, and that's what strategic planning is about. Indeed, performing arts organizations can benefit from what might seem at first like an unnecessary exercise. However, self-reflection and self-assessment—that is to say, the strategic planning process—is not a superfluous exercise; rather, it is an insightful one that leaves the organization and its people transformed for the better. Or, as Roundabout likes to say, it's an exercise that at its heart is "all about you."

As Julia C. Levy, executive director of Roundabout Theatre Company, explains, "Roundabout balances public service with creativity. They are completely entwined. When it comes to producing theater, the number one core mission is to bring great works of art to the stage for artists and audiences, creating a community."

Chapter 7

From Goals to Objectives and Tasks

Now you have a set of lofty goals that are institution-wide and fully endorsed by the staff and trustee leadership. How do you transition from qualitative goals to measurable objectives, broken down as tasks assigned to individuals or teams to be accomplished on schedule and on budget? This is the action planning process in which the strategic planning moves into the various departments of your institution. The result will be an *action plan* that details what staff will accomplish over the planning horizon and addresses the financial, human, and facility resources they need to do the job. This internal working document is formulated by staff with guidance from senior management and the director. The action plan needs to be completed first because without it there is no realistic budget and no assurance that the goals can be fulfilled. It is usually provided in the *workbook*.

This process, which is often neglected, occupies most of the bottom half of the hourglass diagram (steps 7, 8, and 9) and is critically important for aligning the entire organization around the agreed-upon goals and common purpose expressed in the mission statement. Without the action plan, the strategic plan is just another glossy report sitting on a shelf.

A Regional History Museum Prepares Its Action Plan

Let us imagine that a regional history museum has just completed the top half of the hourglass and the retreat. Its mission statement is unchanged:

> To preserve and communicate to residents and visitors the history and creative spirit of those who have lived here from the beginning of human habitation.

On the recommendation of the director, those at the retreat agreed to expand the mandate to include art as well as history, anthropology, and archaeology.

There was consensus at the strategic planning retreat on how to address the lack of audience diversity, static and outdated exhibits, and an organizational structure that reinforces departmental isolation. The recently appointed director presented her strategic planning report at the retreat, outlining the goals she believed essential to turning the museum around:

1. Expand the mandate of the museum to include both historical art and works of art by living artists.

2. Build an addition to create a meeting place for the community, renew the exhibitions, and accommodate new art collections that will be acquired.

3. Encourage risk-taking and creativity among museum staff.

At retreat breakout sessions, participants discussed the key issues and goals suggested by the director. There was consensus on the director's goals, but the retreat participants added two goals:

4. Launch a major project to rename and rebrand the museum, and a campaign to promote the new identity of the museum.

5. Apply advanced information technologies to all aspects of museum work and the way we serve our communities.

So Now What?

The director is understandably excited because the retreat has endorsed the direction she wants the museum to take. She has already started writing the high-level plan that situates the new mandate and the five goals in the context of a community that has changed tremendously since the museum was founded in the 1950s. She has just begun working on the section about the new building addition when she realizes there are some steps, such as a feasibility study, that need to be taken before an addition is announced. So she adds that to her report.

Then she starts writing about why collecting art will have positive effects for the museum and how it will allow them to engage with local collectors and with the indigenous people of that area who produced so much great art. As she is writing, she realizes that in order to fulfill this goal, a few more steps need to be taken. This "writing project" is becoming too big for one person. She has a regular Tuesday senior management meeting the next day, so she puts the problem to the team: "How do you see achieving these goals?"

The chief curator suggests that the goals be handed out to the departments that specialize in each function. He offers to take on the first goal—expanding the collection: "We'll work on a collection strategy and some new job descriptions." The head of buildings and grounds volunteers to deal with goal 5, new technology, and goal 2, the new addition. The director of external relations (which includes development, marketing, and public relations) offers his staff to take on goal 4.

Everyone looks at the human resources manager, expecting her to take on goal 3. She observes that creativity is an issue for every department, not just HR. "It's something everyone has to own," she says.

The director of external relations says, "Taking on art collections will have a huge impact on our fundraising strategy and our membership. We really need to be involved in planning that."

The chief financial officer speaks up, "A new addition isn't just about buildings and grounds, it has capital and operating cost implications. If there is going to be a feasibility study, we should be running it!"

In a few more minutes the following becomes clear:

- All five goals have implications for every department in the museum.

- To fulfill the goals, people have to leave their "silos" and work together.

- The department and division heads cannot create the action plan without input from their staff.

- The departments already have a process for developing plans that ties into the budget cycle; that process could be adapted to the five strategic goals.

And so the strategic planning workbook was invented! There is a booklet and series of templates on the museum computer system that help each department organize its objectives and priorities according to the goals in the strategic plan.

Strategic Planning Workbook

The strategic planning workbook is a tool to guide staff in preparing an action plan to accomplish the goals established by the board. The workbook includes the following:

- The retreat report—that is, any revisions to the foundation statement, the key issues, strategies, and goals as well as next steps.

- Worksheets for those participating in the preparation of the action plan.

The worksheets are organized by goal and have lines for the staff of each department to complete:

- objectives—the short-term quantifiable activities needed to fulfill the goals

- tasks—the steps required to complete the objectives

- person(s) responsible

- resources required (financial, human resources, and facilities)

- beginning and ending dates

- outcomes expected from each objective

- performance measures to determine whether the outcomes were achieved

The more deeply that staff members, who are responsible for delivering core functions of the organization based on policies established by the board, are involved in determining the specifics of the action plan, the more they will be invested in its success and the more willingly and enthusiastically they will be accountable for its implementation.

After each department of the regional history museum had filled in its workbook, the senior management team met for a full-day work session to review and integrate the departmental plans into one master list organized by institutional goals. What they learned was somewhat surprising:

- *On average, about 80 percent of the objectives and tasks that the departments listed on their worksheets were regular functions of those departments—but now they were aligned under institutional goals. For example, external relations always conducted visitor surveys. That was now seen as a task under the objective "Understand the motivations of our visitors and nonvisitors," which supported goal 4 (Branding and Communications).*

- *About 20 percent of objectives and tasks were new activities that required additional financial and human resources. The feasibility study for the new building addition (goal 2) required about $100,000 not currently budgeted. The formulation of a collection development strategy to encompass art and redefine the museum's collection (goal 1) required hiring an adjunct curator and several interns.*

- *Just under half of the objectives were listed by more than one department, even though different departments used different words. For example, visitor research was mentioned by external relations, buildings and grounds, and public programs. Technology training was listed by all departments. And public programs, curatorial, and external relations mentioned initiating a major temporary exhibition that gets people excited about the art and history of the region.*

The senior management team determined the top priorities for the first year and created interdepartmental working committees to lead them.

When the head of finance first added up the costs of the additional projects generated by the strategic plan, the total came to about $1 million in the first year, $600,000 in the second year, and $800,000 in the third year. But when low-priority items were eliminated and duplicate items were removed from

Organizing Objectives and Tasks by Goals

Goal Champion or Lead, and Title:							
Author or Coordinator, and Title:							
Department:							
Goal (#, Description):							
Objective (#, Description):							
Tasks/Steps:	Who will take responsibility for leading? (Name, Title)	Who is responsible for progress monitoring? (Name, Title)	Who else is required to assist or partner? (Name, Title, Internal/ External)	When will this begin?	When will this be completed?	What are the potential resources required? (Technology, HR, Time)	What are the estimated budget requirements?
Expected Outcome:							
Performance Measure (Qualitative + Quantitative):							
Impact Measure (Qualitative + Quantitative):							
Estimated Progress Reports (Month. Year):							

Figure 7.1 Sample strategic plan workbook page. *Courtesy of Lord Cultural Resources.*

training, visitor research, and a few other areas, it was possible to streamline the budget and reduce the total to an amount the development staff thought they could raise.

Following the senior management work session, each department head revised his or her departmental plan to reflect what had been decided on that day.

As a result of the workbook process, the museum had a strategic action plan that included the following:

- *Departmental plans organized by each of the five goals and a budget for each department.*

- *A museum-wide strategic action plan organized by the five goals with about twenty prioritized objectives and one hundred tasks—with budgets and timelines for three years.*

- *Three interdepartmental committees to manage and monitor three major priorities: a feasibility study for the new building addition, a communication and branding process, and information technology initiatives.*

Now the director can write her "big picture" strategic plan in full confidence that the museum staff understands it, they can fulfill it, and the museum can afford it. She will present this plan to the strategic planning steering committee for discussion and approval—knowing that she and her senior managers can explain and defend it. And then the strategic planning steering committee will recommend it to the board for approval.

Facilitating the Staff Process

Many staff members have never had any experience in planning. Their working day consists of tasks. The workbook process provides an invaluable tool in helping staff understand how tasks are linked to objectives and goals that will improve the organization's performance. This can be motivating or tedious—depending on how it is conducted.

Some parts of the institution lend themselves to specific financial or numerical measurements: Has the development department achieved the goals in the plan? (If they haven't, the reasons may lie outside their purview, or there may be internal issues that need to be resolved.) Is the budget balanced at the end of the year, or have there been years of deficits? Do the exhibitions or exhibits open on time? Are exhibition catalogs and labels ready when they do open? If the organization is a research institution, how many new contributions have the staff made recently?

Other objectives may be established, but resources will be needed to measure whether they have been achieved. For example, did visitors learn what we were trying to communicate in this special exhibition or permanent installation? Are resources set aside in the budget to measure this kind of goal attainment?

Staff will have to think about their objectives for the coming year and how they will know if they've achieved them—that is, they will have to define their own performance measures. This is another area where patience and persistence, as well as leadership, are important. Supervisors need to establish measurable objectives and require their staffs to achieve them, reviewing progress against the performance measures on a very regular basis—monthly, quarterly, and annually. Tying the achievement of objectives to the evaluation of staff performance is a critical and effective way to focus attention on the goals and objectives in the plan.

Many parts of the organization are dependent on other parts to achieve their goals. The membership department, for example, may not be able to achieve membership goals with a weak program schedule. The exhibitions office will not be able to print labels on time if the label copy is not received from authors on schedule. Educators cannot create exciting programs or contribute to meaningful interpretation if they are not included early enough in the exhibition planning process. Therefore, each part of the organization needs to develop and plan its work and be evaluated on the achievement of their specific and measurable goals. For example, if label authors are evaluated on the content, style, and timeliness of their label copy, they will have reason to write well and to submit the copy on time. If there are no consequences for missing a timeline or an objective, it will be harder to achieve the results everyone wants. Again, this is why staff should be evaluated on their achievement of results in the strategic plan—it is a powerful motivator in aligning work across the institution.

In order to address these planning issues, establish a task force with five to ten individuals (depending on the size of the organization), representing each functional area. The task force may include the director and senior management team, as in the example above, or the director could guide a task force composed of division directors, department heads, and project leaders. This group coordinates the strategic action plan.

Staff involvement can be organized either by division or by individual departments. In either case, involving everyone in the working group is too cumbersome, so select five or six people who together understand all aspects of the department or division. The process of completing the worksheets usually takes about three meetings.

Meeting 1

Begin by reviewing the responsibilities of the task force and the staff work groups, the schedule, and the process from work group to final decision making.

Discuss the vision, mission, and goals of the organization and the role of the various departments in achieving them. This is an opportune time to air expectations about the role of other departments, not just one's own.

Review the sections of the action plan worksheet and what information is needed. Not everyone will be familiar with the meaning of objectives, outcomes, and performance measures—now is the time to discuss the product the groups are working toward.

Identify volunteers for key tasks, such as recording the discussion on flip charts and providing written summaries. The group may decide to rotate or share these tasks, as long as someone takes responsibility for delivering products that are needed throughout the duration of the groups.

Meeting 2

The purpose of this second meeting is to brainstorm ideas for how the department can fulfill each of the goals. Start by brainstorming the *outcomes*. Outcomes are the changes in behavior—among visitors, stakeholders, donors, staff, volunteers, and so on—you want to see as a result of achieving the goals for your institution. By centering the discussion on the changes you want to accomplish, "out of the box" and collaborative tasks are more likely to arise. After all, tasks are solutions, not just ends in themselves. Record all these ideas on flip charts.

Tasks and performance measures will emerge throughout this discussion, as will ideas for who might be responsible for them. Similarly, record all of these ideas on flip charts using different colored markers.

The ideas on the flip chart will need to be collated. No doubt there will be ideas that are very similar, and these should be grouped. (It is not yet time to edit the ideas.) One or two members of the group will be responsible for putting the ideas together, using the worksheet for each goal as the format. The action plan is beginning to take shape. The draft worksheets should be circulated to all members of the groups in advance of the next meeting.

Meeting 3

The work groups now begin to synthesize the preliminary task lists by consolidating similar ideas and making them more explicit, grouping them by strategy or objective, identifying gaps, and completing the worksheets. Between meetings, members of the group can check in with their departments to get feedback on ideas and suggestions—and to make sure that current and planned tasks and activities are considered.

This is also the time to discuss current activities and to determine whether they serve the new goals of the institution. They may, or they may not. It may be possible to reconceive these activities so that they are aligned with the goals established in the strategic plan. Some activities may need to be dropped. This is one of the hardest parts of strategic planning. However, it is important to free up resources (and reconsider old ways of doing things) to create the needed time, energy, and excitement to implement the action plan successfully. For example, if the strategic plan for your library establishes the new goal of being a leader in community well-being, you may need to eliminate older projects such as exhibits unless you can afford additional resources or establish new partnerships.

While each of the work groups is looking at all of the goals, specific goals may be more explicitly within the area of a particular work group's expertise and responsibility. This is fine.

Amalgamating the Results

The task force (or senior management team) is charged with the responsibility for creating an integrated plan. After the departmental staff work groups have prepared their preliminary action plans, the task force will review the worksheets for each goal to consolidate, refine, and clarify tasks, outcomes, and performance measures. They will also organize tasks by objectives and adjust the assignments of responsibility, the timeline, and the resources. Since each member of the task force participated in the work groups, they can bring to bear a high level of knowledge about the staff's thinking and intention.

The task force will then prepare the draft strategic action plan, completing the editing of the worksheets, and including the following:

- a timeline illustrating the schedule of implementation

- budget requirements

- a process for monitoring the plan by staff, management, and the board

Often, as part of the plan, an organization needs to spend more time evaluating a particular option or potential business model. Some of the best plans include an objective, usually early in the plan timeline, to evaluate the feasibility of some option, such as creating an artist-in-residence program or expanding the physical facilities of the theater. Fully examining the options and deciding which direction to choose requires resources—time, money, and energy. It is particularly important that organizations examine the full range of options, as well as the spectrum of resulting impacts, before making a decision. Transparency and accountability are key to success here. The milestone in this case will be the decision point when one of the options is chosen.

Case Study 7.1

Henry Ford Estate—Fair Lane
A Twenty-First-Century Blueprint for an Iconic Historic Home

Sarah Hill

Built between 1912 and 1916, Fair Lane in Dearborn, Michigan, was the beloved home of Clara and Henry Ford. This large, combination Prairie-style and Romanesque mansion on the banks of the River Rouge—with fifty-six rooms, an indoor pool, massive rose gardens, and a hydroelectric powerhouse—served not only as a family retreat, but as a place to quietly entertain friends like Thomas Edison, Harvey Firestone, and John Burroughs, as well as dignitaries and even royalty.

Globally recognized as an inventor, innovator, and entrepreneur, Henry Ford is well-known for his genius in the development of the automobile and the assembly line process, as well as for his formidable work ethic. However, his interests and opinions extended much further into subjects such as personal mobility, social equity, labor, and the living wage. He was also an outspoken anti-Semite. Clara Ford was active in social and educational issues, and was deeply involved in the betterment of young women, the Henry Ford Hospital and health care system, intercultural movements, and gardening movements. From the beginning, Fair Lane also functioned as an incubator for new ideas and a laboratory for tinkering and innovative thinking.

After Clara's death in 1950, Fair Lane was acquired by the Ford Motor Company—the contents of the home auctioned off or dispersed to family members, and the house outfitted as a corporate headquarters and archive. Six years later, 210 acres of Fair Lane were gifted by the company to the University of Michigan to establish a Dearborn campus on the surrounding farmlands. The house became a conference and community event center, opening occasionally for public tours. In 1966 the estate's historic significance was formally recognized with National Historic Landmark status.

A Strategic Approach to Planning

For decades, the University of Michigan operated the estate as an active community event space and restaurant. In 2010, the estate closed to the public in preparation for a transfer of ownership to a newly established 501(c)(3), to be managed along with the Edsel & Eleanor Ford House in nearby Grosse Pointe Shores. Uniting the two estates under the umbrella of the Historic Ford Estates presented a unique chance to create a critical mass around the Ford family legacy and bring this hidden piece of national heritage back to life. However, this opportunity was also accompanied by a set of real challenges, including extensive restoration work needed to return the estate to the historical period of 1912 to 1932, a backlog of repairs and maintenance inside and out, the absence of original furnishings, limited public awareness of the estate beyond the immediate region, and, unlike the financially independent Edsel & Eleanor Ford House, no endowment to contribute to restoration or operating costs.

Another challenge, perhaps even more difficult to tackle than the condition of the estate, was the character of Henry Ford himself. How could the estate accurately reflect and objectively interpret the multifaceted Henry Ford—his sometimes contradictory personality; his many roles as husband, father, man, tinkerer, innovator, and businessperson; and his controversial opinions and practices—to achieve credibility as the authority on all things Ford? And, how could the estate ensure that his narrative would not overshadow Clara's story and her significant contributions to human well-being?

It was clear to President Kathleen Mullins and the executive staff that developing a new future for the Henry Ford Estate and successfully tackling these challenges required a strategic approach and the creation of a detailed action plan to guide activities and investment over the next five years and beyond.

Reimagining the Henry Ford Estate

Facilitated by an external consulting firm, the executive team, along with the board of trustees, embarked on a strategic planning process. Research and analysis, a series of interviews with board members and key informants, and collaborative workshops with executive staff identified an important opportunity for rethinking the traditional historic house experience, the restoration process, and the role of Fair Lane locally, regionally, and nationally:

- Instead of velvet ropes and docent tours, could visitors be encouraged to sit down, make themselves at home, and explore at their leisure?

- Rather than closing the estate for restoration, could public viewing of the conservation work be used to promote stewardship and to become a hands-on teaching and training opportunity?

- While domestic life at Fair Lane would undoubtedly be of interest to visitors, could the estate's narrative be widened to elevate Clara Ford's story to greater prominence and to promote and perpetuate the couple's greater contributions to American industry and society?

- In focusing on a wider story, was the estate prepared to address and openly discuss some of the more contentious aspects of Henry Ford's personality and history in order to inspire a national dialogue, to act as a catalyst for meaningful debate around issues still relevant today, and to stimulate innovative solutions to these problems?

Through additional benchmarking research and study visits to some of America's top historic houses, the executive team began to formulate a clear vision for the estate, with ideas about how to bring this vision to reality. The executive staff worked closely across their respective departments to craft aspirational institutional statements and strategic directions, and after further refinement at a planning retreat with the board four strategic directions were confirmed:

1. *Historic House Redefined.* Revitalize the estate as a leading historic home experience that meets the needs of a twenty-first-century audience, utilizing the restoration process as a platform for engagement to promote and encourage stewardship.

2. *Dynamic Story.* Increase awareness and deepen understanding of the legacy of Henry Ford, while elevating Clara's story to greater prominence to reveal new narrative layers for a more dynamic and engaging visitor experience.

3. *Strategic Alliances.* Develop strategic alliances with individuals, organizations, institutions, and companies that match the spirit and ambition of the Clara and Henry Ford legacy in order to position the estate for success.

4. *Solid Foundation.* Build a sustainable organization.

A home is a place of comfort and safety, but in many ways it is also for self-expression. With this philosophy in mind, the executive team further underpinned these strategic directions with a strong set of organizational values inspired by those of Clara and Henry Ford themselves—integrity, experimentation, simplicity, excellence, and action. These values would embolden the estate every day to be true to the Fords' spirit in their approach to issues, their choices, and their behavior. The estate would not shy away from some of the more contentious issues of their history and personalities. Instead, they would commit to being open and straightforward in all things, placing decisions and actions in their historical context to build understanding, while initiating meaningful and constructive dialogue in order to move the conversation forward.

Journey Toward Success

With mission, vision, and mandate firmly in place, a commitment to openness and honesty, and a series of key strategic priorities, the executive staff set to work devising the specific and quantifiable objectives necessary to establish a comprehensive but realistic plan of action. Over several months, twenty-two objectives were identified, detailing how the estate would successfully realize this vision and achieve each of the four goals.

Arriving at and agreeing on this course of action was not a simple process. Executive staff faced many obstacles in the development of their objectives. As is the case with heritage restoration projects, a plan of action had to be established while much of the action was already underway. Akin to hitting a moving target, some objectives were being crossed off the list just as quickly as they were being written down. Additionally, the complexity and unpredictability of the restoration process often turned up new research or complications that required changing an objective or rethinking certain aspects of the plan. Flexibility, adaptability, and an understanding that plans are living, breathing documents were key to finally pinning down a set of objectives.

Another hurdle was the scale of development and the level of activity required to get the estate, the visitor experience, and the organization operational on a solid footing. By working collaboratively across departments, executive staff began to recognize how interconnected all aspects of the undertaking were—restoration, interpretation, staffing, and fundraising. Changes or prioritization in one area would have knock-on effects elsewhere. Therefore, the executive team had to make serious collective decisions about which objectives to prioritize in the short, medium, and long term to ensure balance across departments and to build capacity across the estate.

Finally, the toughest challenge in translating goals into actionable objectives was maintaining a high level of ambition and optimism while being realistic about what could be achieved in the next five years given the expenses required, the estate's financial situation, and staff capacity.

The renaissance of Fair Lane signals a new era in the history of the Henry Ford Estate. With a strong set of institutional statements and values, a solid strategic plan, and an annual update of the actions required to fulfill the plan, the estate moves closer and closer to becoming the leading authority on Clara and Henry Ford and to building a strong and authentic foundation for the future. By committing to and engaging in the strategic planning process, the Henry Ford Estate is now positioned to take its place among America's iconic historic properties.

Figure 7.2 Perhaps more challenging than improving the estate's condition was determining how to accurately reflect and objectively interpret the multifaceted and controversial personality of Henry Ford. *The Historic Ford Estates, Grosse Pointe Shores and Dearborn, Michigan.*

Chapter 8

Implementing the Plan

The planning process can be a powerful launch pad for organizational renewal. After the planning process is complete, everyone should have a greater understanding of the mission. The staff and board should now be committed to achieving the agreed-upon goals. Staff morale should improve with better communication between board and staff. The strategic plan is a road map for moving everyone forward together.

This chapter looks both internally and externally to keep the strategic planning documents "off the shelf" and available to everyone in the organization, to foster alignment across the institution, and to communicate the exciting plans to the widest possible audience.

Detailing the Plan

Progress toward goals is possible only if specific and measurable objectives have been established at the outset. This can be challenging for staff, especially if they are not used to setting measurable, time-specific objectives. The workbook described in the previous chapter establishes the overall objectives for the plan. The next section describes how to implement them.

A good way to stay on course for the annual goal is to set quarterly objectives, which staff may devise themselves or which may be determined by supervisors. Supervisors can then track progress toward the objectives every three months with their personnel, identifying any problems or needed revisions. This fairly frequent review regularizes the process. It becomes part of normal institutional life and therefore less intimidating to staff, as it allows early and minor course corrections rather than more draconian changes.

At Hillwood Estate, Museum & Gardens, heads of each division report to each other on their progress toward the strategic plan's goals twice per year. The halfway point serves as the first cross-divisional check-in, simply because the first quarter's performance is usually not sufficient to assess progress. This six-month report gives the group a formal setting to hold each other accountable for parts of the plan that directly affect other museum departments. The formal oral report to a peer group provides added incentive to complete the objectives on time. The reporting

Table 8.1 Example of an implementation planning worksheet.

Objectives and Tasks	Measurement	Priority	Lead and Participant	Start/Finish	Resources	Issues or Concerns
1. Review target audiences (including tourists) and define success in reaching them. Marketing, with input from all divisions, will develop a matrix itemizing all current audiences, assigning overall institutional priority to each audience group and identifying lead department(s) for cultivation of each audience group. In addition, consider the following tasks specific to existing major audience groups:			Marketing Education Development	By 9/1/06		
a. Reach more traditional cultural users.						
i. Continue institutional advertising program and consider expanding to WETA or WAMU (local radio stations).	Paid admissions increase by 5 percent per year regardless of programming	High	Director of Marketing	FY06–Ongoing	$200,000 per year for advertising (in operating budget)	Uncertainty of operating funds for advertising
ii. Formalize collection of e-mail and mailing addresses at admissions desk.	Goal of 20,000 e-mail addresses institution-wide; weekly report	High	Visitor Services	FY05-06/06 and ongoing	$1,500+ for computer and volunteers	Need plan for management of database

Strategy/Action	Measure	Priority	Responsible	Timeline	Funds	Challenges
iii. Seek empty-nesters through targeted promotions with specific publications and downtown properties.	Voucher or discount offer is redeemed and tracked	Medium	Group Sales	FY06, ongoing	Funds needed to print coupon offers	Staff time: detailed promotions are time-consuming
iv. Seek members of the gay community through special promotions and events (include possible tourism tie-ins).	Track membership and admissions	High	Group Sales	FY06	About $15,000 for ads	Can this be tracked?
b. Increase tourism visitation through marketing collaborations.	Out-of-state participation measured by data collected on site	High	Director of Marketing			Uncertainty of funds to continue tracking
i. BACVA (Approach for Gee's Bend joint campaign)		Low	Director of Marketing	03/07–09/08	Regional ad, co-op money via grants?	
ii. Mt. Vernon Cultural District high-end luxury customer packaging	One per month?	High	Group Sales	06/04–ongoing	MVCD membership	
iii. Area hotel packages	Track concierge vouchers	High	Group Sales	07/04–07/06		Reporting system?
c. Grow family audience through increased membership sales targeted to families; add games(s) to the website.	Increase family memberships, paid child attendance	Medium	Membership Marketing	FY06?		System must be adapted to carry different membership categories

process provides a natural forum for working through what can sometimes be difficult problems. Over time, the working group becomes more comfortable talking about tough issues and more sensitive to the needs of other parts of the institution, as well as more aware of the contributions everyone makes to the whole enterprise.

Reporting on progress toward goals continues the cycle. It is wise to follow the principles of transparency and accountability throughout the process. If everyone is aware of goals and objectives, if they are discussed on a regular basis throughout the year—at board meetings, at an all-staff meeting, at board committee meetings and meetings of various volunteer committees—and if each person knows what part he or she plays, the goals are much more likely to be achieved. Moreover, if underlying assumptions have changed or if an objective or task has proven to be ineffective, changes can be made. The plan needs to be a living document, not a straitjacket.

The Financials in the Plan

An important part of a complete strategic plan is a yearly schedule of the resources necessary to carry out the major objectives, along with an assessment of whether those resources can be obtained within a given timeframe. One way of doing this is to note, on the more detailed work plan, the resources needed for each objective. Dollar amounts will begin as rough estimates, but, as time goes on, yearly budgetary needs can be specified. The key is to understand competing needs for resources and to determine the priority of each. Create an understanding throughout the organization about how to balance priorities.

The feasibility assessment may also be fairly rough in the early stages of the planning process and in the early years of the plan. If a large capital campaign is envisioned, a detailed fundraising feasibility study is usually needed and should be scheduled as a milestone within the plan. The result of that study will influence the decisions and actions that follow: Is there enough enthusiasm within the constituency for a major expansion? What are the highest priorities of the members and donors, and do they coincide with those of the organization's leaders?

When there are multiple objectives, the senior management team will have to compile a "wish list" with the financial requirements of each item. They can then consider capital, special project, and operating needs over the life of the plan and begin to prioritize funding the competing objectives. It is also wise to develop a five- or ten-year plan for ongoing capital needs, regardless of where those needs are eventually placed in the list of priorities. Boilers and chillers have a lifespan, as do roofs, computers, and servers. Planners need to look forward to see what capital reserves will be needed to maintain the technical infrastructure and the physical plant.

The Budget and the Plan

There will be a point at which the plan is approved, usually at a full board meeting. Then it is time to put the plan into action. The annual budget should reflect the goals and objectives announced in the plan. In other words, the budget is the plan outlined in yearly financial terms and thus the budget must be aligned with the plan. If this is not the case, the staff will realize it first, and the board soon thereafter; in time, the community will sense that what the organization says is disconnected from what it does.

The underlying principle in creating a budget is resource allocation. Since resources are finite, an organization makes choices between many possible ways of deploying its resources. A budget is

Table 8.2 Five-Year Capital Spending Plan.

	Year 1	Year 2	Year 3	Year 4	Year 5	TOTAL
Roof replacement		162,800				162,800
Copper roof replacement				500,000		500,000
Roof replacement—West Building		82,000				82,000
Replace air handler—West Building			25,000			25,000
Replace air compressor—Building 1			25,000			25,000
Replace air compressor—Building 2			10,000			10,000
Replace air compressor—West Building			10,000			10,000
Chiller overhaul 1				8,500		8,500
Chiller overhaul 2					38,000	38,000
Chiller overhaul 3				32,000		32,000
Boiler overhaul 1					33,000	33,000
Boiler overhaul 2			1,600		1,700	3,300
Boiler overhaul 3			1,600		1,700	3,300
Boiler overhaul 4			1,600		1,700	3,300
Repair and paint exterior wood, windows, and brick			1,400		1,500	2,900
Seal Limestone Cupola Building	56,000	44,000				100,000
Paint interior—offices—materials only			25,000			25,000
Paint interior of West Building—offices—materials only		6,000				6,000
Overhaul elevators—Building	2,500	7,500				10,000
Overhaul elevators—Building					10,000	10,000
Overhaul elevators—West Building			15,000			15,000
Repair or replace AHU 4 and AHU 5 ductwork installation				5,000		5,000
Increase boiler room air make up			37,000			37,000
Screen wall renovation			10,000			10,000
Security equipment upgrades and replacements	100,000					100,000
Furniture: office equipment replacement		5,000	5,000	5,000	5,000	20,000
Overhaul water booster pump system		3,000	3,000	3,000	3,000	12,000
Cost to vacate Engineer Club space	7,000					7,000
Contingency projects	20,000					20,000
Annual totals	33,500	25,000	25,000	25,000	25,000	133,500

the final determination of how financial resources will be allocated to departments and projects. Management determines the institution's tactical progress toward its strategic direction through the budget.

Usually, the budget planning process for the coming fiscal year starts six months earlier. Here is a typical schedule:

As staff members begin to prepare their budgets for the upcoming fiscal year, they should consult the plan, noting the resources they need to achieve the year's milestones and refining the estimates included in the workbook. Supervisors should check that the budget accurately reflects the resources to be devoted to achieving their area's objectives.

When the finance director receives all of the departmental (or divisional) budgets and has the income projections for the coming year, he or she will know if departments need to revise their budgets to match expenses with resources. Senior management then confers with the finance director and the executive director to resolve any disparity. The finance director may have suggestions; there may be ways to "value engineer" projects, to partner among divisions, or to conserve resources. In most cases, there are not enough resources to do everything every member of the staff would like to do each fiscal year. In recent years, many organizations have had to cut back their budgets as a result of tightening economic conditions. A good plan, based on a thorough process, will guide resource allocation and indicate where budget cuts will be less harmful to the organization. For example, if "outreach to the community" is one of three major objectives over the next few years, choosing to make cuts first to the education division's staff may indicate a misalignment of resources to goals.

The director has the overall responsibility to ensure that the institution's resources are aligned with the plan, while the board, as the fiduciary, must also determine that resources are being deployed appropriately to achieve the stated strategic goals.

Progress on the strategic plan can be tracked with a yearly schedule, beginning at the end of the budget planning timeline set out above:

June: Fiscal year budget is adopted at board meeting.

July: Finance department issues budget to all staff members, with quarterly allocations for each line.

Monthly, throughout the fiscal year: Departments receive reports of budget variances and meet with their supervisors to discuss if necessary.

September: Senior managers meet with board strategic planning committee to lay out the large yearly objectives (this can happen earlier in the fiscal year if enough key players are available).

Early October: Staff meets with supervisors to report on first quarter progress.

Early January: Staff meets with supervisors to report on second quarter progress.

Early February: First year-end projections are prepared by finance department. Senior managers report to each other on progress to date, suggest course corrections, and discuss large budget variances and year-end projections that need to be addressed.

Early April: Staff meets with supervisors to report on third quarter progress; finance department prepares year-end projection; additional course corrections devised, if necessary.

Late May: Senior managers meet with board strategic planning committee to report on fiscal year accomplishments and projections for year-end.

June: Staff meets with supervisors to report on fourth quarter progress; strategic planning committee reports on current fiscal year progress to the full board.

In the second half of the fiscal year, rolling out that year's budget overlaps with planning for the upcoming year. Keeping a keen eye on progress being made toward objectives within the current fiscal year and the state of the current-year budget makes accurate forecasting of the next fiscal year's budget more likely, although it is usually challenging no matter how careful one is.

Alignment with the Organization's Long-Range Plans

The strategic plan forms the base for the development of many other organizational plans. For example, a master plan for buildings or landscaping can extend over many decades. Similarly, initiating a playwriting competition, a collections plan, or the creation of a digital library could have quite a long timeline. All of these plans should align because their guiding force is the vision for the institution manifest in the strategic plan.

Organizations have varied histories, and plans may be developed in differing sequences. Perhaps an institution starts by deciding it needs a new building to better serve its community. This may be the catalyst for taking a deeper look at its role in the community; that, in turn, could spark a strategic planning process. Knowing where you want to go and what you want to be in the future is critical to making good decisions about your building. What programs might you want to provide? For whom? What size do you see your audience becoming? All of the questions you answer as part of the strategic planning process inform your architectural plan as well. Launching a master building plan without the foundation of a strategic plan leaves many of these critical questions unanswered, and the results are likely to be disappointing.

Alignment with Human Resources Strategy

How the organization wants to relate to its community is often reflected in its human resources strategy. Staff, board, and volunteer diversity is crucial to maintaining a strong institution that reflects the community it serves today and in the future. Strategic planning goals related to diversity and inclusion need to be aligned with the human resources strategy of the organization. Those goals are much more likely to be achieved with a robust and diverse staff and board.

Board composition can also be fine-tuned with the strategic goals in mind. If a building is planned, for example, major donors will be needed. Board members with a deep understanding of the building trades and urban planning may be helpful. If a major shift in creative strategy is envisioned, board members who have experience with successful business innovation can provide vital insights. Aligning the work of the board nominating committee to the strategic plan will result in a board with the competencies required for better decision making.

Alignment of Staff and Board

The strategic planning process leads the board and staff to agree on the strategic goals for the organization. This alignment should be reinforced over the years the plan is implemented. A yearly face-to-face presentation is an effective way to communicate to the important internal constituencies of staff and board. The director can launch the new fiscal year by sharing an executive summary of the goals and objectives to be addressed in the coming twelve months. Some organizations hold an annual meeting with all of their members. Staff and volunteers are motivated by knowing they are receiving the same presentation given to the board of trustees. This ensures alignment across the organization and helps everyone to relay the same message to external constituencies. Doing this in person allows the director to field questions and hear concerns directly. Having real communication with your closest constituents reinforces their importance to the organization. This kind of communication takes time, patience, and effort—but nurturing these relationships builds strong organizations.

Frequent communication also reinforces alignment. Staff members can report on their part of the strategic plan at board meetings, where a give-and-take dialogue can take place. Board committee meetings provide another forum for discussing progress. The more frequently board and staff confer about progress toward their shared goals, the better.

The Public Dimension: Communicating the Plan

The strategic planning process communicates out as well as in. You can be sure that the workshops and interviews—both internal and external—will have raised expectations among stakeholders, patrons, and community members. Artists are wondering if you are actually going to implement the artist residency program discussed in one of the workshops. Politicians are curious about whether there is a new building in your future, and preservationists are worried about how change might impact a historic site. Teachers are concerned that you will charge more for school visits. You will, of course, have sent thank-you letters to all who participated in your consultation process, letters that promise that there will be a public presentation of the plan and that participants will receive a copy. We now focus on using the public document as a communications and marketing tool and on aligning it across the institution.

There are a myriad of ways to communicate an institution's vision and strategic goals. You can prepare a stand-alone print piece that can be distributed to high-level members, press, funders, and community leaders. The text is usually written by the director or by the communications department in consultation with the director; the piece includes plentiful photographs and illustrations so readers can better understand your organization. This is a high-level document, brief and to the point, that states the mission, vision, mandate, and strategic goals in plain language, avoiding insider jargon. The document may also highlight some of the key projects (or objectives) that you plan to achieve during the planning period. It does not include human resources or budget information. These can be appended to the plan when shared with funders and donors. This public document should acknowledge all of those involved in the plan—board members and committees, community leaders, and participants and staff. This demonstrates the depth of the planning process as well as the breadth of the community involved in crafting the strategy.

Having a printed piece that can accompany funding requests underscores the intentionality of the organization and how the particular request fits into the overall plan. It can be a powerful statement of the organization's commitment to its goals and its community service.

Many institutions also share this high-level strategic plan on their website. Each year, progress toward the goals can be shared as various objectives are achieved and milestones reached. This transparency serves an organization well as everyone can see how activities fit into the overall plan. Many times, those closest to an organization—its members, donors, volunteers, staff, and board—appreciate seeing this transparency the most, and it can motivate them to deeper engagement and commitment. They share in the institution's pride and can more deeply own the institution's success. It may make sense for cultural organizations to commission a film or video about the plan. Communication should not be one-way, so think about how people can comment on the strategic plan and provide feedback.

Case Study 8.1

A Great Garden of the World: Our Planning Story

Paul B. Redman

Longwood Gardens' legacy is as rich and beautiful as the historically and artistically acclaimed Brandywine Valley of southeastern Pennsylvania where the gardens are located. Longwood Gardens is the result of the vision of one man, Pierre S. du Pont (1870–1954). From the time Mr. du Pont was a young man, he envisioned having a world-class display garden that would be open every day of the year. He purchased a small farm and well-known arboretum in 1906 and set about fulfilling his dream. While others of his era were building tall walls to keep people out of their beautiful properties, he built a garden that was never to have walls. Today, Longwood is known around the world for its stunning horticultural seasonal displays, extraordinary gardens created by some of the greatest landscape designers of the twentieth and twenty-first centuries, global plant research, and educational programs that are developing future generations of horticulturists and public garden leaders.

Fifty-five years after Mr. du Pont's death, it was time to renew his vision for Longwood Gardens to ensure that it remained a relevant, world-class garden in the twenty-first century. In 2008, for the first time in Longwood's history, a comprehensive strategic planning effort was initiated with the help of external consultants. The quantitative results from that planning effort were real: a 109 percent increase in earned revenue, a 79 percent increase in attendance; and a 306 percent increase in the number of member households. However, the real impact is less tangible: evolving an internal culture that pushes for leadership and innovation at all levels, establishing a golden rule of delivering an extraordinary experience, creating new universal performance measures, and establishing a new vernacular based on our shared values and vision. Some people have called the new language "Longwoodian."

Even with the amazing success that we experienced from the initial strategic plan, we learned a few lessons on our planning journey.

1. Invest time to create shared understanding.

Even though we had an inclusive and transparent planning process, we learned that you do not just roll out the plan and say, "It's time to make it happen." You must invest time on the front end to create as much understanding as possible within all levels of the organization. One of our key planning principles is "it begins at the top." The board of trustees, chief executive officer, and senior executive team members live and breathe the plan and keep it front and center at all times. In addition, ongoing communication is paramount. We accomplished this through many channels, including by reorganizing our governance structure to monitor progress and alignment of resources and via our meeting forums, which ranged from large town-hall gatherings to one-on-one meetings.

2. Connect the dots and reinforce the path.

Strategic plans can be intimidating and difficult for many to grasp. It is easy to get wrapped up in the long list of tasks and lose sight of the big ideas. Our staff town hall meetings provided one of the most effective ways to reinforce our mission, vision, values, and strategic plan. The dots of our vision and the tasks being carried out every day are connected at the beginning of every town hall meeting agenda with an open forum during which any staff member or volunteer can take the floor to publicly acknowledge accomplishments or victories. Every victory can be connected to outcomes articulated in our strategic plan. Another powerful tool for connecting the dots is the internal PLOG (Paul's Blog) that I write. The theme of each post can be connected to our strategic plan, mission, vision, or values. Over time, the collection of short essays has become an important resource for staff and volunteers.

3. Terms and words are powerful and must be embraced by all.

We establish an entirely new Longwoodian vocabulary in our strategic plan with powerful words like "intellectual capital" and "curatorial voice" that were difficult for many of the staff to implement. We hit the pause button on implementation of the plan and engaged staff in special focus-group sessions that produced priceless feedback that helped define these new terms in the voice of the staff and not in the voice of the consultants or executive leadership. The powerful *Working from Our Values* document was developed as a tool to build skills and to onboard new staff. It provides a foundation for discussing everyday work behavior that aligns with our values and behavior that does not align with our values.

We also developed an entirely new annual individual performance review tool that reinforces our mission, vision, values, and strategic goals. After these two new strategic performance tools were created, we developed internal training courses that every staff member was required to finish before completing the new individual performance self-review. Grounding the performance review in our vision, values, and goals opened the door for a formal, annual discussion about our strategic plan between supervisors and their direct reports.

Strategic planning documents and, in particular, the task worksheets can be overwhelming because of the amount of information that is presented. We learned the importance of

Annual Evaluation Period	10/01/15 – 9/30/16
Employee Name and Current Job Title	
Manager's Name	
Overall Rating for the Year	

SECTION ONE:
EXPERTISE AND MODELING OF OUR CORE VALUES
(See next section for tasks in support of strategic goals)

How have you demonstrated Longwood's Core Values in your job tasks?
Core values: Excellence, Fiscal Alignment, Stewardship, Community Engagement, Leadership

Self-Review:

Manager's Comments:

SECTION TWO:
TASKS IN SUPPORT OF OUR STRATEGIC GOALS
(If there is a goal that you did not have a task and/or accomplishment under please leave that goal blank.)

Strategic Goal #1
Evolve the organizational and financial structures to ensure that Longwood Gardens achieves its mission.

Self-Review:

Manager's Comments:

Strategic Goal #2
Achieve an extraordinary guest experience.

Self-Review:

Manager's Comments:

Strategic Goal #3
Develop a curatorial voice and program plan to create a cohesive experience.

Self-Review:

Manager's Comments:

Strategic Goal #4
Help establish innovative environmental stewardship practices for public gardens.

Self-Review:

Manager's Comments:

Strategic Goal #5
Expand learning opportunities and share intellectual capital with the world.

Self-Review:

Manager's Comments:

Figure 8.1. Longwood Gardens performance review tool. *Courtesy of Longwood Gardens.*

SECTION THREE:
EMPLOYEE PROFESSIONAL DEVELOPMENT
(Training, Conferences, Seminars and Workshops Attended, Recognition, etc., Please include resources needed and time frame when possible.)

Progress made during the current evaluation year:

Plans and suggestions for the upcoming year:

SECTION FOUR:
ACTION STRATEGY FOR NEXT YEAR
Outline FY2017 employee goals in support of the **2016 - 2022 Strategic Plan**

Action Strategies for FY2017:

SIGNATURES:

I understand that my signature indicates only that I have read and discussed this performance evaluation with my supervisor. It does not necessarily mean that I agree with the evaluation's contents. I may attach written comments, if desired.

Employee: _____   Date: _____

Manager: _____   Date: _____

PERFORMANCE RATING SCALE:

1. Exemplary (Truly outstanding performance that results in extraordinary and exceptional accomplishments with significant contributions to Longwood's objectives. Work is always timely, and always of exceptionally high quality. People at this level always model all of the Core Values in a way that inspires others.)

2. Very Good (Often generates results above those expected of the position. Contributes in a superior manner to innovations both technical and functional. Work is nearly always timely and of high quality. People at this level consistently demonstrate all of the Core Values.)

3. Satisfactory (Acceptable performance. Employee fulfills all position requirements and may on occasion generate results above those expected of the position. Work is nearly always timely and of quality. People at this level reliably demonstrate the Core Values.)

4. Needs Improvement (Weak performance. Employee sometimes fails to meet position requirements and/or sometimes fails to demonstrate Core Values. Work is sometimes late and of poor quality.)

5. Unacceptable (Unacceptable performance. Employee consistently fails to meet position requirements and/or fails to demonstrate Core Values.)

Figure 8.1. *(continued)*

creating sound bites for our most recent 2014 strategic plan to create a greater understanding of the strategic themes and priorities. For example, themes from our strategic plan are "Master Plan," "Information Technology," "Guest Experience," "Fiscal Flexibility," "Civic Responsibility" and "Mission Impact."

4. It's not about doing more and adding more work.

After we launched our first strategic plan, we realized that anxiety was building within the staff because they were focusing on the long list of tasks in the strategic plan. Communication and dialogue were the answer. We engaged staff in classic "stop, start" discussions, which helped them understand that the strategic plan was not a list of more work to do but instead was a tool to help them make decisions about doing the most important work and discarding the work that was no longer relevant. As a result, we became more efficient, innovative, and productive.

5. Be realistic and don't develop a "to do" list for tasks.

We were told by our consultants not to be aggressive or too lofty with our tasks. In the end, we were lofty and had a very aggressive strategic plan, which added another layer of anxiety to the staff when it came time to implement the plan. Thankfully, we didn't fail and we advanced every goal, but the process was tiring and sometimes resources were not in place to support a specific task. As a result, when we developed our next strategic plan we included an entire year of launch strategies prior to the strategic plan to ensure that our pacing was realistic, that ownership of the tasks was understood, and that our resources, both human and financial, were aligned in advance.

Figure 8.2 The Topiary Garden at Longwood Gardens. In 2006, Longwood embarked on a comprehensive strategic planning effort to ensure that it remained a relevant world-class garden in the twenty-first century. *Copyright Daniel Traub.*

Strategic planning is hard work, and we have learned that the most difficult part of planning is task development and completion of the task worksheets. These processes can be tedious, and all of us at Longwood understand why many strategic plans fail at this point. We strive for trust, engagement, and delegation to get the best ideas and ownership throughout all levels of the organization.

The development of the overall strategic plan is delegated to a cross-departmental staff steering committee, and the development of strategic tasks is delegated to cross-departmental task development committees. Each task development committee is composed of representatives from the staff steering committee as well as additional staff; these committees are assigned to develop tasks for a specific goal. This is a highly effective way to develop tasks because the very people responsible for implementing the plan are informing the development of the tasks that will be included in the plan. If the members of the task development committee are doing their job well, they are serving as ambassadors for their departments and getting feedback from their colleagues. In addition, the cross-departmental representation on the committee identifies potential overlaps as well as new synergies within the organization.

The list of tasks in our first plan—a plan that had incredible results for us—was exhausting. It was a comprehensive, detailed, point-by-point list from A to Z of specific actions that were to be implemented. They were all important tasks, but in the end it was a specific "to do" list—and for five years we managed the A to Z "to do" list successfully. However, we learned there was a way to make implementation of the strategic plan more successful.

6. Focus on the idea of the task and what you are really trying to accomplish.

When it came time to develop the tasks to support the goals of our new strategic plan, we had an "a-ha" moment. One of the biggest barriers to implementing the plan was the simple question by frontline staff: "How do my annual goals and daily duties fit within the strategic plan?" We realized that rather than developing an exhaustive and detailed list of tasks, we should focus on the idea of what needed to be accomplished to achieve a goal or objective. Our tasks in the new plan are clear, but they are broad enough that any staffperson at Longwood can align his or her annual performance plan with the strategic plan. In addition, focusing on the idea of the task creates flexibility within the plan that diminishes the possibility of a task becoming irrelevant or not happening. Developing tasks that are "idea outcome" oriented also opens the door for innovation, enhances dialogue among and within departments, and serves as a gateway to identify future leaders.

Strategic plans require an enormous commitment within an organization. However, the benefits of planning can be exponential if the plan is successfully implemented. For Longwood Gardens, the keys to successful strategic plan implementation are inclusiveness, trust, delegation, a safe environment for discussion, simple terminology, and a big communication toolbox to continually reinforce the vision and ideas of the plan. We have discovered that by following these principles you can achieve lasting, laser-like focus that will provide you with returns, both tangible and intangible, never before imagined.

Chapter 9

Evaluating the Strategic Plan

"Are we there yet?" Many of us can still hear those tired voices on the family road trip.

Having worked so hard to produce the best—most inspiring and practical—strategic plan ever, we still need a dashboard to tell us where we are on the trip, how much energy we have used, and which if any goals we have achieved. How can you evaluate the progress your organization has made toward the goals in the plan? And more broadly, how can you evaluate whether the overall goals in the plan are still relevant to the circumstances? To keep the road trip analogy going: Should you make a detour?

The Board's Role in Evaluation

Although it is important for the staff to measure progress against objectives in the plan, as described in the previous chapter, the board is responsible for working with the director to evaluate the progress toward the goals and to make sure that the institution is on the right road. The strategic planning committee of the board has an important role to play each year throughout the life of the plan. The committee assures the full board that the strategic direction is being carried out in the operational objectives and tasks of the staff. To do so, the board's strategic planning committee (which includes the director and some executive staff) could meet at the beginning and end of each fiscal year. As a practical matter, these meetings can be merged into one in which last year's results and the upcoming year's objectives are discussed, or the recap can take place at the end of the fiscal year and the forecast can happen in the first quarter.

The director and executive staff who are accountable for the various deliverables in the plan lay out what they aim to accomplish in a meeting with the strategic planning steering committee at the beginning of the fiscal year. To keep the meeting to two or three hours, each division should present in very broad terms what it plans to accomplish in the current fiscal year. Staff should convey only the "big ideas" and not the operational minutiae, as that will result in glazed eyes and a ten-hour meeting. This may take practice; it is a good idea for the staff to rehearse the presentation with the director to get feedback before the meeting with the board committee.

A good strategic planning committee avoids "meddling" in the staff's work but is not afraid of challenging them to be more effective in achieving goals. Board members are there to check on progress toward the agreed-upon goals, not to lobby for specific pet programs or to direct operations. If the staff presents appropriately, these complications are far less likely. If the director and board chair (the cochairs of the strategic planning steering committee) are working together, they can take "the view from five thousand feet"—where there is enough texture to understand but not enough detail to meddle.

At the end of the fiscal year, staff should report on progress toward goals and objectives, indicating what revisions were made along the way. In addition to assuring the board that the strategic direction they adopted is being carried out within the budget parameters, this process gives board members the opportunity to discuss changes that may need to be made. It also creates a board that is better informed about the way the institution works and the problems it is facing—and it may inspire them to provide more resources to solve those problems.

Often, board members well versed in business methodologies can help staff answer the "so what" question. Does the strategy you have chosen really make a difference? How can you tell? Does it move you toward your goal? What impact is it having on the community? What metrics will help you measure your achievement? What are you choosing not to do? Although these questions can be hard to accept at first, answering them focuses the staff in a positive way.

Here is an example of a strategic planning committee's report to the full board, after the board and senior staff have had their reporting meeting near the end of the fiscal year.

Strategic Planning Steering Committee Report

We just completed the first year of our strategic plan. We defined three big goals:

- Be known for contributing to the well-being of our city.

- Boost the creativity of our programming.

- Increase the diversity of the staff and board.

The staff has made significant progress in each area, working on about twenty objectives. While we have yet to see the needle move decisively, we believe that our institution is on the right track. Here are some of the measures for the key objectives:

Be known for contributing to the well-being of our city.

- Mentions in the media. Our institution has been continually in the news, with fifty mentions this year compared to twenty last year. Last year we were in the arts and social sections of the media. This year, the additional thirty mentions were in the news section and business pages. Our development staff members believe that this new profile will attract more sponsors and philanthropic support in the years to come.

- New partnerships in the human services sector. Our executive staff are participating on the boards and board committees of the city's housing authority and on the board of a nonprofit dedicated to immigrant resettlement, and some of our new staff are active in faith-based poverty reduction groups. Each of these partnerships is raising money so that members can attend our programs, thus boosting attendance slightly and significantly diversifying our audience.

Boost the creativity of our programming.

- Number of new commissions. We have commissioned five new works for the next three years: two from local artists, one from a nationally known artist, and two from international artists. For the national and international artists, our staff has partnered with international organizations to share costs and enhance promotion.

- Reviews in national, local, and international media. Positive reviews of the two shows we have had this year attest to the creativity of our programming and helped to drive attendance.

- Educational activities supporting these initiatives. Each of the shows had a series of educational programs aimed at different segments of the audience (families, adults, students), and attendance at these programs tracked against projections. The family festival day outperformed, showing that there is significant untapped potential for us with this segment.

- Tracking changing patron demographics. We are working on baseline audience demographics, creating good metrics to demonstrate changes and investigating software that will help us track demographic markers. So far, we have anecdotal and visual evidence that our audience is diversifying as well as increasing.

- Patron survey results. We trained volunteers to capture demographic and satisfaction data from our patrons. While this process has not been without its challenges, we now have a core of capable volunteers whose data we can rely on. We have only been able to complete one survey this year, during a family festival, and 85 percent of attendees were "satisfied" or "very satisfied" with the experience.

Increase the diversity of the staff and board.

- Diversity of staff and board. The attached chart compares diversity by human resources (staff) and nomination committee (board) over a three-year period. We are doing better at diversifying our staff than our board, but our governance committee is committed to continued progress in this area.

- Diversity compared to peer institutions. The attached chart compares our data with regional and national data. We are not yet leaders in the field but we will continue to strive to be.

- Engagement of diverse staff and board on committees (trustees) and projects (staff). We are reaching out to nonboard committee members to cultivate potential new board members by involving them in our work. We have already made great progress in populating projects with diverse staff, continuing the momentum that was started in the cross-divisional meetings we had in the strategic planning process.

Involving All Board Committees

Each board committee, in addition to the strategic planning committee, has a role to play in assuring the success of the strategic plan. Each board committee should review the plan during the year, following the strategic planning committee model but going deeper in the area of its responsibility.

The finance committee reviews the upcoming year's budget and ensures that resources are aligned with the plan's goals and objectives. In addition, during the year, they check to make certain that budget variances are properly dealt with. The committee may ask, for example, that staff prepare a contingency plan early in the year to be put into place if soft income does not materialize by a certain date.

The development committee plays an important role in seeing that the organization raises the funds it needs for priority projects; their work may help determine if a capital or endowment campaign is needed. The marketing and education committees support those parts of the plan that deal with the audience response to the institution. Therefore, they have an important role in asking critical questions throughout the year to ensure that the museum stays aligned with its strategic direction. They may also ask for metrics from comparable institutions to determine if the organization is serving a sufficient number of schools, for example, or offering enough adult classes.

The governance committee houses many board-specific objectives—for example, identifying and attracting appropriate new board members and ensuring that they are thoroughly oriented to the museum's mission, mandate, and strategic plan.

Staff Roles in Evaluating the Plan

Each staff member should have objectives and duties aligned with the strategic plan. Managers will have very specific, measurable objectives that guide their work, and their success in achieving them will define their contributions to the organization. They can align with the plan the weekly, monthly, and quarterly reports they provide their supervisors. The more closely the work of the organization is aligned to the plan, and the better the performance measures gauge the achievement of the objectives, the more progress the whole organization will make toward its goals. Measuring outputs and outcomes will let an organization know where it stands; the sooner missing objectives can be identified, the sooner course corrections can be made. Although staff may only report to the board a few times each year, they should be keenly aware throughout the year of where they stand in achieving the objectives. Having senior managers report to each other halfway through the year on their objectives is a good way to check alignment against goals and objectives. This also improves communication, surfaces smaller issues that may be slowing progress, and may spark discussion on larger emerging issues. Six months is enough time to have made some progress, to forecast where the institution will be at year-end, and to make larger changes if needed to balance the budget. A half day should be set aside for a thoughtful discussion; a timed agenda can be used to keep everyone on track, and short visual presentations organize the data to be communicated.

The Bigger Question: Are These the Right Goals or Is It Time for a New Plan?

The governing body constantly evaluates the institution's achievement of its mission. Because it is not involved in daily activities, the board can see the larger picture and assess whether the organization is true to its purpose. Further, the board should assess whether the organization is efficiently and effectively serving its purpose, but it should not micromanage the process of doing so. This assessment is a serious duty; therefore, boards should meet regularly in executive session to conduct this discussion. Often, though, because staff members are most conversant with changes in the field, they sense first that it is time to refresh or rethink the strategic plan. Large conferences can also play important roles in forecasting for the field, spotlighting innovations and trends, and allowing everyone to learn what peers are doing.

Staff, if they are attuned to their metrics, may also be first to know how audiences are responding to the institution's offerings. They should also know how their organization stacks up against others in their region and across the nation. As everyone in the field defines and assesses success more effectively, crafting the organization's unique value proposition and ensuring that it still resonates with the institution's audiences becomes more important.

Change is constant. Museum staff and board leadership are expected to understand and respond appropriately to change. Knowing when and how to alter direction and when to stay the course is an attribute of outstanding "visionary" leadership. The tools that strategic planning provides are accessible to everyone and help cultivate leadership throughout all levels of the organization, potentially resulting not only in visionary leadership but also in a cultural institution that makes a difference in the community and the world.

Case Study 9.1

Measuring What Matters in Strategic Planning

Veronica Y. Blandon

Metrics can drive performance and accountability at all levels of an organization and can ensure that strategic planning will lead to action, progress, and the attainment of goals. For metrics to be effective they need support from staff, leadership, and the board of directors. They also need to provide management with insight into the organization's performance in relation to strategic goals. A clear link between metrics and strategic goals ensures that staff and management are *measuring what matters*. Thus, the metrics an organization develops are as unique as the institution being evaluated.

Measuring Impact

Increasingly, funders are requesting not-for-profit organizations to report on their impact and to build a business case that demonstrates their value to visitors, stakeholders, and the community. Furthermore, board members want to understand how the organizations they lead are making a difference within the communities they serve.

As a result, metrics can measure the achievement of objectives like ticket sales, revenue, and institutional growth. They can also determine the impact of an organization's strategic goals, mission, programs, and activities.

Measuring impact captures the results of the organization's efforts and raison d'être. Nevertheless, defining and measuring the influence of a not-for-profit organization is difficult.

It requires an in-depth understanding of the organization's mission, functions, and strategic goals, as well as the way its offerings are perceived, both internally and externally.

There are numerous methods by which to measure impact. However, there is no one-size-fits-all methodology. Existing methods cannot fully contend with the complexities of cultural organizations. They are narrowly focused and program or activity specific. Therefore, they are not able to capture all of the benefits that cultural organizations provide to stakeholders and the community at large.

While facilitating various strategic plans over the course of the past six years, we realized that cultural organizations needed a methodology to measure the impact of their strategic plan. More recently, clients began to approach Lord Cultural Resources to help them demonstrate the impact and return on investment they are making to private and public funders. In 2015, we began working with the Royal Conservatory of Music (RCM) to do just this. The need for a standardized methodology that could also be tailored specifically to RCM led to the development of a new model for measuring impact well suited to strategic planning.

Outcome and Indicator Model for Measuring Social, Cultural, and Educational Impact

What is social impact? In the for-profit sector, companies provide stakeholders a return on their investment by way of stocks and dividends. In the cultural sector, institutions provide stakeholders with value via their offerings: collections, programs, exhibitions, and facilities. Thus, social impact is the *value* or *benefit* that not-for-profit institutions provide society.

For metrics to be useful, they need to evolve with the institutions they measure. Cultural organizations have expanded their role. Today, they are influential civil society institutions that provide exponential benefits to numerous stakeholders. These benefits can be categorized into five types: social, cultural, educational, environmental, and economic. Unlike environmental and economic impact assessments, social, educational, and cultural impact assessments are relatively new.

Table 9.1 illustrates an outcome and indicator model that provides a standardized approach for capturing and measuring social, cultural, and educational impact by identifying outcome themes for each. Outcomes are changes in behavior that visitors, stakeholders, donors, staff, or volunteers experience as a result of the activities and programs the institution provides and the goals it achieves. The assessment begins with an examination of the organization's programs and offerings and identifies stakeholders. For each outcome theme, several indicators are used as qualitative and quantitative metrics to calculate the value stakeholders gain by interacting with the organization.

Royal Conservatory of Music

The Royal Conservatory of Music (RCM) is a legacy institution that has been developing human potential through leadership in music, the arts, and education in Canada since its inception in 1886. "The Royal Conservatory of Music is one of the largest and most respected music education institutions in the world, providing the standard of excellence in

Table 9.1 Outcome and indicator model for measuring impact. *Courtesy of Lord Cultural Resources.*

Impact Type	Outcome					
Cultural	Tackling Unemployment in Culture	Improving Innovation	Enhancing Equity and Diversity	Increasing Access	Improving Local Image and Identity	Fostering Personal Empowerment
Social	Increasing Social Cohesion and Inclusion	Strengthening Public Life	Building Safer Communities	Improving Health and Well-Being		
Educational	Enhancing Knowledge and Understanding	Improving Attitudes and Values	Enhancing Activity, Behavior, and Progression	Increasing Enjoyment, Inspiration, and Creativity	Building Skills	Providing Lifelong Learning

curriculum design, assessment, performance training, teacher certification, and arts-based social programs."[1]

In 2015, RCM commissioned consultants to conduct a review and assessment of the scope and scale of its social and related economic impact to demonstrate to private and public funders the benefits of their contributions.[2]

The goals of the study were as follows:

- Gain an understanding of RCM's financial position and model and how it compares to others.

- Assess RCM's seven public programs and offerings and identify its stakeholders, the benefits they experience, and the value they receive as a result of RCM's programs.

- Quantify RCM's impact.

Our analysis demonstrated that the RCM has an extensive impact on one in seven Canadians with its public programs. RCM's stakeholder groups reach across the country and deep

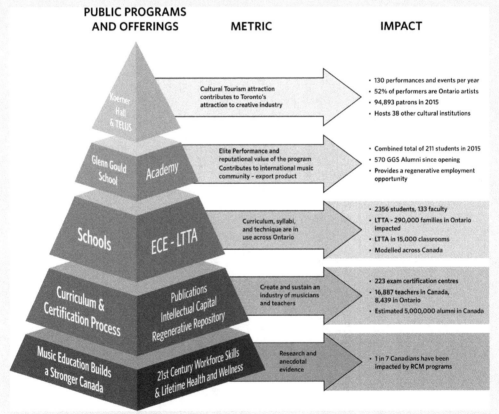

Figure 9.1 Measurement model developed for the Royal Conservatory of Music. *Courtesy of Lord Cultural Resources.*

into communities from urban centers to rural areas. RCM truly lives in people's homes and communities as illustrated in figure 9.1, on the previous page.

While RCM is justly famous for its superb Koerner Hall for performing arts and its Glenn Gould School for Elite Performers, the study demonstrated that RCM's exam and certificate program has the broadest reach and impact on students and teachers across the country, and it provides music teachers with a significant economic benefit. These results are detailed below.

The social impact assessment revealed a direct correlation between certification and a regenerative employment opportunity that contributes to music teachers throughout Canada. Simply put, music teachers with RCM affiliation earn higher wages than those without the same training and affiliate status, providing an economic boost to smaller communities.

The methodology employed to estimate the labor market impact associated with RCM uses data and information from a variety of sources. Music teachers with some level of RCM certification were assessed in various industries based on the North American Industrial Classification System (NAICS). Data for average wage and hours worked were obtained for these industries and averaged to determine a proxy for the average hourly wages for music teachers with RCM certification. Comparing the average hours worked and average annual

Figure 9.2 Historic home of the Royal Conservatory of Music. *Image credit: Daderot.*

Table 9.2 Quantitative and qualitative benefits of RCM. *Courtesy of Lord Cultural Resources.*

Social Impacts	**1. *Changing lives through sustained exposure*.** The RCM certification system has produced an estimated five million alumni in Canada (two million in Ontario) that have collectively engaged in tens of millions of contact hours as individuals progress through the ten levels of instruction.
	2. *Social and community cohesion where people live.* The Presence of RCM, through its certification systems and RCM-affiliated music professionals in communities across Ontario, creates long-term nodes of social cohesion that enrich lives and foster creative connections.
	3. *Diversity and range of partnerships that leverage RCM's program reach and strengthen local networks.* RCM works extensively with more than thirty-eight cultural organizations to make accessible, high-quality performance spaces and to implement 235 teaching and examination centers across the country.
Cultural Impacts	**4. *Contributing to the vitality of the Canadian music industry as a whole.*** RCM is widely credited by musicians who attest to the central role it has had in their achievements. Notable alumni credit their professional success to RCM's training, and more than 40 percent of 2015 Juno[1] nominees have an RCM affiliation.
	5. *Building cultural tourism.* Koerner Hall is widely recognized as one of the greatest performance venues in the world, enhancing Toronto's reputation as a destination for music and cultural tourism.
	6. *Fulfilling Ontario's cultural mandates with exceptional quality and a high profile*. At each level of government, RCM aligns with key economic and social goals that support strong growth.
Educational Impacts	**7. *Supporting the validity of music education as a keystone for academic and personal achievement.*** The range of RCM programs and their lasting effects, from research to arts education in the classrooms of underserved youth, leads to a stronger Ontario.
	8. *Building and sustaining the Canadian music teaching industry.* RCM affiliation has a verifiable positive economic impact on the capability of professional music instructors to earn a living teaching music.
Financial Performance	**9. *Diversity and strength of its business operations, contributing to a stable and strong business model that effectively leverages government funding.*** An analysis of provincially funded peer institutions reveals that RCM is grounded on a diverse range of revenue sources, with an emphasis on earned sources from six lines of business. Earned revenues for the RCM represented over 65 percent of total revenues, far exceeding the comparative range among peer institutions.

salary data to the average salaries of individuals with just a high school education allowed the consultants to calculate a wage differential that is, in part, due to the music education that RCM helps enable. The average wage differential was then multiplied by the number of active music teachers with RCM certification to obtain an estimate of the labor market benefits facilitated by RCM.

The RCM Certificate Program (and its component curricula and examinations) forms the foundation of professional music instruction as a creative industry in Ontario and Canada. RCM affiliation has a verifiable impact on the capability of a professional music instructor to earn a living teaching music. The RCM's affiliation contributes an estimated $5,292.50 to each teacher per year. This results in a staggering economic contribution of $63,510,000 to 12,000 teachers in Ontario, and $129,137,000 to 24,400 teachers across Canada.

Thus, the certificate program promotes the local economy by providing employment opportunities with superior wages for affiliated music teachers while encouraging the sales of learning materials and instruments.

The study demonstrated that the Royal Conservatory of Music is truly a high-impact cultural asset fulfilling its mission to "develop human potential through leadership in music and the arts—based on the conviction that the arts are humanity's greatest means to achieve personal growth."

Notes

1. Royal Conservatory of Music (RCM), "Overview," www.rcmusic.ca/overview.

2. The consultants were Lord Cultural Resources and Collins Barrow.

Case Study 9.2

Using Metrics to Further Alignment at Hillwood

Kate Markert

Marjorie Merriweather Post, heir to the Post cereal fortune, bought Hillwood in 1955 and soon decided her home would be a museum to inspire and educate the public. Her northwest Washington, D.C., estate endowed the country with the most comprehensive collection of Russian imperial art outside of Russia, a distinguished eighteenth-century French decorative art collection, and twenty-five acres of serene landscaped gardens and natural woodlands for all to enjoy. Opened as a public institution in 1977, Hillwood's allure today stems from the equally fascinating parts that make up the whole. From the captivating life of Marjorie Post to the exquisitely maintained mansion and gardens, the experience of Hillwood leaves visitors enchanted.

The mission of Hillwood Estate, Museum & Gardens is "to delight and engage visitors with an experience inspired by the life of founder Marjorie Merriweather Post and her passion for excellence, gracious hospitality, art, history, and gardens." Post was known for her exacting standards, so the zeal for perfection throughout the estate is part of its DNA and is shared by board and staff.

In 2011, Hillwood adopted a strategic plan based on a strategy of exciting special exhibitions that would promote attendance from June to December, beyond the traditional high spring season when the gardens are at the height of their bloom. One goal was consistently to achieve seventy-five thousand visitors (up from a high of fifty thousand) and to increase knowledge about the estate. Other objectives included establishing a three-to-five-year exhibition schedule and the infrastructure to support it, creating and maintaining partnerships to further the mission, maintaining scholarly excellence, increasing philanthropic support, and maintaining the campus to Post's standards.

By 2015, attracting seventy-five thousand visitors per year had become the "new normal," with an exhibition schedule that included "Wedding Belles: Bridal Fashions from the Marjorie Merriweather Post Family, 1874–1958," "Pret-a-Papier: The Exquisite Art of Isabel de Borchgrave," and "Cartier: Marjorie Merriweather Post's Dazzling Gems." Even though five years had not elapsed since the major goal had been achieved, the plan needed to be updated.

The board and staff agreed on one major point: ever-increasing attendance was not in the best interest of the visitors or the estate. Hillwood is a particularly intimate experience, a wonderful oasis in the heart of Washington, D.C. Its charm would be destroyed if a visitor no longer felt like one of Post's guests, allowed to linger in awe of the Fabergé Eggs and to stroll at a leisurely pace in the gardens. Through a series of discussions, board and staff agreed that the next phase of Hillwood's development would instead focus on the quality of the experience, deepening engagement with visitors, members, donors, board, and staff alike.

The first step was discussion at each of the board committees: governance, collections and programs, buildings and grounds, finance, and development. Senior staff and board members reviewed what had been accomplished in the first strategic plan and proposed ideas for moving forward. Staff collected the notes from those meetings in a white paper that was shared with the board and the full staff. Based on the deep shared understanding of how Marjorie Post lived at Hillwood and her high expectations about how guests would experience her collection and gardens, there was agreement that an ever-increasing number of visitors would not achieve the mission of "delighting and engaging" them. A consensus emerged, culminating in three major goals: (1) deepen Hillwood's engagement with visitors, members, donors, colleagues, and virtual visitors while maintaining a consistent onsite attendance of seventy-five thousand or more; (2) deepen engagement with board, staff, and volunteers through meaningful, efficient, and effective work rooted in the mission of founder Marjorie Merriweather Post and in clear and transparent communication; and (3) maintain and enhance Hillwood's financial health, professional reputation, and campus to comport with Marjorie Merriweather Post's standards while serving contemporary audiences in an exemplary manner.

How could that engagement be measured to determine if it was deepening? It is much easier to measure quantitative objectives than qualitative ones. Each department within the organization gathered to brainstorm appropriate milestones. For visitor services, total attendance of seventy-five thousand was an obvious quantitative performance measure, but there were many related measures: increasing off-season attendance by 5 percent, increasing exhibition attendance by 5 percent, collecting e-mail addresses from 50 percent of visitors, receiving 95 percent positive visitor feedback, and increasing repeat visits by 3.5 percent. Development crafted performance measures to increase total memberships from twenty-five hundred to four thousand by the end of the plan, increasing renewal rates of current members to 75 percent, and increasing the number of higher-level donors and exhibition sponsorships, with specific numerical goals each year. Evidence of "deepening engagement" with the gardens is a bit harder to quantify, but it is reflected in increasing attendance at talks and tours of the garden, increasing numbers of workshop participants, increasing numbers of garden volunteers and garden docents, and increased longevity of volunteers and docents with Hillwood.

The first draft of the plan had many gaps in performance measures. Learning to think very specifically about how success will be measured took time and focus. Supervisors worked with their staffs to refine both the objectives and the performance measures, and checked on progress quarterly. Senior managers also reported to each other six months into the year. This allowed enough time to make adjustments, and it gave everyone the opportunity to understand how events across the institution could impact their area. Senior managers were able to make suggestions, sometimes outside of their own bailiwick, about useful performance measures. Incrementally, we began to make progress.

Sometimes, performance measures were aspirational. For example, the goal of increasing repeat visits assumed that we were collecting the relevant data. That required implementing a new ticketing system and training frontline staff on the system and how to interact with visitors to collect the data. It made sense to establish a performance measure, but we also needed to develop a system to know how we were doing. One of our performance measures became to establish baseline statistics for our performance measures across the board.

Social media statistics abound: number of hits on the website, number of friends on Facebook, number of Twitter or Instagram followers. A more vexing problem is how to measure "engagement" on social media and how that translates into affiliation with Hillwood. One of our performance measures is "an established, actionable mechanism for measuring rate of engagement." The objective is to use information from our ticketing system and Google Analytics to better understand how the quantity and type of visits and the frequency of follow-up communication leads to repeat visits, program participation, and membership. It's a tall order, and definitely aspirational, but it is the crux of our work to engage our visitors.

The goal of more completely engaging internal constituencies has led us to become much more aware of how we interact with each other as a board and staff. This goal is rooted in the deep concern Marjorie Post had for her staff: she expected exceptional performance, and she cared for and rewarded her staff in ways quite beyond the norm, giving them lovely wedding gifts, writing notes when they lost a pet, making arrangements for their families to see the estate, just to mention a few examples. It is also grounded in the deeply held belief that extending engagement among the board and staff is the most efficient way to achieve any other goal the institution sets.

What kinds of objectives and measurements will inspire this engagement and show when it is occurring? Our board president very much wanted board members to attend programs at Hillwood, beyond regular board and committee meetings and gala events, and she established an objective to achieve this. She felt it was important for board members to meet Hillwood visitors and members and to see the work of the staff firsthand in lectures, family days, workshops, and tours. It is relatively easy to establish who has attended which events in the past and to determine if more board members are now coming. It has taken leadership from the executive committee to show up for events and reminders at board meetings and in written communication to keep focused on the objective. All this effort has begun to achieve further results: a board better acquainted with Hillwood's work and more inspired to support that work financially.

Many objectives in the plan relate to deepening the staff's engagement, and there are associated performance measures to check on our progress. One objective that has had significant effects is the implementation of a supervisory development program designed to give managers the skills to foster engagement, performance, and retention. In order to achieve this objective, we committed funds in the operating budget to support it. When there are many competing projects, it can be difficult to find funds for staff training. However, because it is so integral to the overall strategy in this plan, it became a priority for funding. The training has inspired managers across the institution to communicate more effectively with their staffs and to align all of their work and weekly reporting to the strategic plan.

Figure 9.3 The challenge was how to frame an evaluation system for the strategic plan of the lovely Hillwood Estate and Garden pictured here. Hillwood Estate, Museum & Gardens, *2014 photo by Maxwell MacKenzie.*

Chapter 10

Conclusion

What Can Go Wrong and How to Fix It

This manual has emphasized that strategic planning is a process with certain steps and characteristics, but it varies from organization to organization and from community to community. Here, by way of conclusion, are some frequently asked questions and the authors' best answers.

How do you make time for planning?

Often, people feel they have so many ongoing projects that they can't take the time for planning. This is, of course, exactly why it is so important to step back, evaluate what is most effective and efficient, and decide what programs could perhaps be eliminated. As the economic environment has become more difficult and the number of staff members has been reduced in some organizations, the stress of maintaining complex programs has become more acute. So the need for planning and priorities is very great, but the problem remains: how can time be made for planning?

Leadership, usually the director and board chair, must begin the process. The director needs to require the staff to take the time to plan. Sometimes planning can be accommodated by pushing some programs into the future or reducing their frequency rather than eliminating them. For example, a permanent collection rotation that is not light-sensitive could stay up for a year rather than being changed every three months; lectures could be held once a month rather than every week.

The key is to make planning a top priority and to work other projects around it. Decide on definite dates and times for meetings and retreats and let go of some other meetings—or have them occur less frequently. Make the commitment of time and financial resources to create a plan.

My board chair doesn't believe in strategic planning. How do you persuade leadership that it is time for a new plan?

Most of the time, people do not want to engage in a planning process, especially an open process that invites a lot of comments from "outsiders," because they are afraid of the risks. So the key is to minimize the inherent risks and to demonstrate that the benefits of planning outweigh those risks.

To begin, you have to admit there is some risk to planning, especially to inviting participation in the process. But there is also risk in not planning, and that may be a greater risk to the institution in the long term. Understanding the organization's place in the community and how to enhance it is almost always worth the time and energy it takes to study it. By doing so, you can respond with more attractive offerings or a more responsive artistic practice that increases the value of your cultural organization to a greater number of people.

Second, you need to persuade the leadership that the benefits outweigh the risk. What potential gains are there for your institution and the community if new ways of thinking are adopted? What risks are avoided by engaging in a planning process?

Finally, you need to develop situation-specific strategies to minimize the risks. For example, one theater was worried that if it offered reduced-price tickets to students, the theater would be asked to fund transportation to get them there. How could this risk be minimized? Teachers who were included in the discussion came up with creative funding ideas whereby they could own the initiative.

There is also the issue of timing. It may take time to persuade leadership of the need for planning and to devise methods to mitigate the risk. Or it may take a change in leadership for serious planning to occur.

We have a plan that's on the shelf. How do we make the plan part of institutional life?

This is best accomplished from the top down, but there are also decentralized ways to promote a plan. The plan is more likely to become integrated in the life of the institution if the board asks for a yearly progress report. Even better if the board asks at the beginning of the fiscal year for a forecast of what will be accomplished during that year and then hears a summary of progress at the end of the year. That way, yearly financial goals are more likely to be linked to goal setting.

The director may also use the plan to align the activities of the whole staff and to make sure that each person understands his or her part in achieving the institutional goals. The more the plan is talked about—in staff meetings of all sorts, in the annual report, on the website, and in other contexts—the more it guides decision making and daily institutional life.

If leadership is not promoting the strategic plan, senior staff may take the initiative to use the plan in their regular reviews with staff and to make reports about their division's progress to their peers and to the director. Often, one senior manager reminds the group to tie the plan back to discussions about operating issues. If the plan had the support of everyone when it was conceived, gentle reminders can be very helpful in maintaining focus.

We're starting a planning process but are afraid that if we include our community, they will want things that we can never provide. How do we manage their expectations so they aren't disappointed with the final plan?

This is basically an accountability issue. Even if the institution is unable to respond to all requests from the community, thorough and careful reporting to the community will lead to greater success. You can let people know at the outset that you want to hear what they have to say, even if you are not in a position to deliver on each and every idea. Then, be sure that community members understand what you did with the information and that it was thoughtfully considered, among many other ideas. The outcome can be posted on the website or published as a concise report to the community about the future direction of the organization.

People understand that resources may be constrained and that management will have to make choices among many good ideas. Some may have to wait until next time, and the report can indicate this. This open process may also allow you to ask for financial support for ideas that the community wants but for which there are no funds at present.

We are interviewing people in the community, but the only people we know are fans. How do we get more diverse responses?

It may be a hard lesson to take to heart, but you do not necessarily learn much from people who agree with you. Your institution will be strengthened by knowing what key leaders—funders, church members, community activists, or corporate leaders, for instance—really think of you. However, you have to be willing to hear constructive criticism and differing points of view.

Which opinion leaders are most important to hear will vary with the institution and the community. For a children's garden, a group of single mothers may be the most important. For an industrial museum, the leaders of the local labor union may be relevant.

Discovering the key opinion leaders should be fairly easy. However, they will be extremely busy, and their time should be used carefully. They should receive a letter, signed by the director and board chair, saying that they have been selected for an interview and introducing the outside consultant who will call to make the appointment. The letter should outline the three or four key questions that will be asked; the interview itself should take thirty to forty-five minutes. Often, a telephone interview is the best way to obtain candid feedback.

The board is asking for goals that we have no possibility of achieving. How do we develop more realistic, achievable goals?

The staff responds to every suggestion by saying that we don't have the human or financial resources to carry it out. How do we learn to stretch as a staff? Where do we find the balance between unrealistic expectations and not pushing hard enough?

These are two sides of the same question. The resolution rests in part on a thorough understanding of the institution's historical data and its local environment, as well as comparative measures from similar environments around the world. The size of audience and amount of income possible in New York or Toronto are not comparable to what can be achieved in Hartford or Owen Sound. Beware of assuming that everything will change radically with a new strategic direction. Change usually takes longer than anyone expects.

Plans based on the idea that "miracles happen" without relevant data supporting that assumption can lead to catastrophic failure. On the other hand, not dreaming big enough can lead supporters to abandon an institution that lacks aspirations. To know what is reasonable, the organization must understand its numbers: How many visitors are there, and when do they visit? How much do patrons spend on admission? (The average admission price can be shockingly lower than the adult admission charge when children, members, tour groups, and discounts are figured in.) How much do they spend on merchandise? How much has been donated in annual grants, gifts, previous capital campaigns, and so on? Only with this information can projections of future income be made with any accuracy.

Having staff attend conferences on a regular basis will ensure that throughout the institution people are aware of best practices in the field and that they are networked with their peers.

Bringing in a consultant who has helped other institutions deal with similar issues ensures an objective outside view of what is reasonable. Such a perspective can persuade either an irrationally exuberant board or a timid staff that there is a viable middle ground.

Providing a forum where all sides of the issue can be thoroughly discussed allows anxieties to be aired and, perhaps, sights to be raised. Sometimes the larger goal is possible over a longer time horizon. Sometimes having respected peers talk to the board and staff will help all sides gain some perspective.

Here are some pitfalls to avoid:

1. Cookie-cutter goals. These are not based on the specific situation but look like every other cultural organization's strategic goals.

2. Fantasy goals. These are not based on current, reliable data. They are "wishful thinking" and unachievable from the outset. An example is to assume that if it can be done in New York, it will work anywhere.

3. "Silo" goals. Instead of looking at the whole institution's direction, the plan immediately divides into functional area goals—artistic, education, curatorial development—without thinking about cross-cutting issues that pertain to the institution's overall performance and how every part of the organization can contribute to the achievement of that goal.

4. "Softball" goals. This is the opposite of fantasy goals—here the institution opts for business as usual and doesn't challenge itself to stretch further.

Is it really important to include financials in the plan?

Without a financial plan, it is impossible to put the narrative into action. The planning process must result in a budget in order for its goals to be achieved. Without the financial plan, it is impossible to know whether the goals are even possible.

That said, it is almost impossible to fine-tune the financials over a longer time horizon. Inevitably, things change from year to year, so the strategic plan financials need to be "order of magnitude" figures that allow the organization to make decisions about general direction during the planning period of three to five years. Then, fine-tune both the financial plan and the work plan in the yearly budget cycle.

The financial assumptions need to be based on real data and not wishful thinking. "Build it and they will come" is a strategy that has recently brought several institutions to the brink of bankruptcy. In making financial plans, have worst-case scenarios that are actually the worst case, then create plans to deal with such outcomes.

Including financials in the plan also ties the plan to the yearly budget process. If the yearly budgets do not reflect the priorities set out in the plan, plan and action are disconnected, and the board should ask why that is so.

Whose responsibility is it to see that goals are achieved?

It is the director's responsibility, but he or she needs to delegate to various members of the management team. If, for example, the education department is responsible for the outreach deliverable, the head of education needs to ensure that the education staff work closely with the development division to achieve that goal. At the same time, if social media staff are responsible for the communication deliverable, they have to work closely with the marketing department to succeed. As individual departments understand that achieving their goals requires the cooperation of other departments, they will also discover how their timely cooperation is critical to others achieving their goals.

How do you constitute the strategic planning steering committee? Everyone wants to be on it!

It is tempting to appoint lots of staff members and lots of board members to keep the peace and avoid offense. This makes it extremely difficult to schedule meetings and usually ensures that the board will have less say in the outcome.

A better solution is to keep the committee to fewer than twelve members. Work back and forth with senior managers, keeping them in the loop and asking them to respond to documents that come out of the planning meeting. Have discussion sessions with larger groups of board members to keep them informed. Report on progress at regular all-staff meetings and at full board and board committee meetings during the planning period.

Too many staff people in the strategic planning committee thwart community input and the "outsider's" perspective that the board brings. Staffers tend to dominate the sessions because they have much more detailed knowledge than others. That prevents the board from functioning as a board and setting the direction of the institution.

On the other hand, a board that does not want staff input can also derail the process. It takes a strong director and consultant to bring in the staff perspective and assure the board that the plans are achievable. Formally bringing responses to proposed plan scenarios from staff members can provide a "reality check." Usually, some board members can also help ensure that the staff perspective is respected.

My manager wants to "observe" our staff workshop. I won't feel comfortable speaking my mind if she's there. How can this be changed?

A consultant can be of great help. The consultant should tell the director and senior managers to resist the impulse to sit in on the staff discussions, precisely because the staff will assume that the managers are going to monitor what is said and guide the discussion to the outcome they prefer.

Staff at all levels should be encouraged to participate in the discussions. Since security and front-line staff often have direct contact with visitors and what they are saying about the institution, their schedules should be arranged to allow them to attend the sessions (even if it means having a manager stand at their post!).

The head of the board planning committee insists on writing his own goals for the institution, even though they are too detailed and don't cross divisions. How do we work with this?

Although the best and most easily remembered plans focus on three to five goals, having a more detailed plan is not catastrophic. However, the director and consultant should work to achieve a compromise that everyone can live with. It is important, though, that the major goals are institution-wide and that all divisions can participate in them.

Who should be invited to the retreat? What can go wrong with too many? Too few?

The retreat should be larger than the strategic planning committee but kept to a manageable number, depending on how many facilitators there are. There should be more board members than staff members in the group.

If too few people are chosen to participate, there may be little reason to conduct a retreat rather than simply meeting as a committee. If many people are invited but only a few are able to attend, that may indicate a lack of support for the institution, its current administration, or the planning process.

Too many people at the retreat will result in the frustration of many not being able to speak or participate fully. A retreat implies seriously grappling with options for an institution's future, and those invited to engage in the process should be seriously committed to it, either as board members or senior staff.

We hope this Q & A has been helpful as you formulate your strategic planning strategy. We wish you great success in steering the future of your cultural organization.

Glossary

The following is a glossary of commonly used terms in strategic planning for cultural organizations. Most of these terms are more fully described in the text.

360-degree perspective. The idea that each perspective matters and strengthens the final result.

Accountability. Indicates that those responsible are required to account for their actions; a clearly anticipated process will be available for inspection, and the reasons for decisions will be explained.

Action plan. A document that details year by year, department by department, what staff will accomplish over the planning horizon and that addresses the financial, human, and facility resources needed to complete the tasks.

Administration. The facilitation of progressive interaction among a cultural institution's functions toward achieving agreed-upon goals and objectives.

Baseline. An organization's actual or current results for a particular performance measure.

Benchmarking. An in-depth process of identifying, measuring, and comparing successful ideas from other institutions to gain insights that will help an organization improve its own performance.

Best practice study. Comparative analysis of outstanding successes in specific programs or activities in other institutions.

Board (or trust). A fiduciary body to whom the public interest in the organization may be committed. The body is to administer the organization with the same diligence, honesty, and discretion as prudent people would exercise in managing their own affairs.

Budget. A financial plan, usually covering one year, with funds allocated to attain the organization's objectives.

Business plan. A document that projects the financial viability of a project under certain conditions or assumptions, which, in the cultural context, may include creative content; a public programming plan; statements of mission, mandate, and purpose; recommendations regarding institutional status and structure; space and facilities requirements; staffing requirements; market analysis; marketing and operational recommendations; projections of capital and operating expenditures and revenues; and an implementation schedule.

Collection policy. A cultural organization's fundamental document governing the scope and limitations of its intended collection, together with standards for its acquisition, documentation, preservation, security, and management.

Common interest group. People linked through a mutual concern or commitment.

Control. The monitoring of budgets and schedules by management to ensure that resources of time and money are utilized in accordance with allocations.

Effectiveness. A qualitative measure of the extent to which the organization's efforts achieve the intended results.

Efficiency. A quantitative measure of effectiveness in proportion to the effort—in person-hours, money, space, or facilities and equipment use—required to achieve the relevant outcome.

Environmental scan. The initial step in a strategic planning process, which aims to develop an understanding of changes in the external environment affecting the institution directly and indirectly, such as economic, demographic, community, market, and professional issues, taking into consideration local, regional, national, and international trends and developments.

Evaluation. Qualitative and quantitative measurement of programs in relation to their objectives.

Extension. Programs that institutions offer outside of the organization's building or site.

External assessment. An effort to see the organization as others see it and to learn from this outside perspective through such means as visitor surveys and consultations with community leaders, donors, sponsors, funders, frequent users, and nonusers.

Feasibility study. A determination of the viability of a proposed institution, or of the further development of an institution, including financial feasibility, marketing prospects, funding sources, visitation and revenue projections, structural suitability of an existing building, viability of various proposed sites, and other factors. This is usually undertaken by specialist consultants independent of the project itself, with a view to making explicit the conditions under which a proposed project may prove viable, usually not in terms of a profit-making or break-even budget, but rather in proportion to the requirement for subsidy, endowment, or other sources of contributed income.

Focus groups. Discussions among representatively structured groups directed by a facilitator to evaluate actual or prospective products or services.

Goals. The long-range qualitative standards or levels of program fulfillment or achievement toward which the organization is striving.

Governance. The ultimate legal and financial responsibility for an institution.

Governing board. The group of trustees appointed to assume fiduciary responsibility for the organization by reviewing and determining policy and long-range plans, assuring adequate funding is in place to fulfill the mission, and engaging, evaluating, and, if necessary, terminating the employment of the director.

Hierarchy. Any organizational structure in which lower levels of responsibility and authority report to higher levels, resulting in a pyramidal structure culminating in the director.

Implementation. Allocating time, money, and staff to accomplish the institution's goals and objectives according to agreed-upon priorities, assigning responsibility, and reallocating or acquiring new resources.

Implementation plan. A coherent plan put together by senior management that integrates all departmental input to coordinate the achievement of goals through multidepartmental teams and within budget constraints.

Institutional context. Issues related to the organization's relationship with other institutions and agencies, including all levels of government, educational institutions, other similar organizations, specialist groups, the tourist industry, and potential donors or sponsors in the private sector.

Institutional plan. A strategic planning document that examines and makes recommendations for both the internal organization of an institution—such as its governance structure and statements of mission, mandate, and purpose—and its external relations with government, educational institutions, other similar organizations, the private sector, tourism, and so on.

Internal assessment. The process of gathering opinions about an organization's present performance and future direction from those closest to its operations: staff, board, volunteers, donors, and members.

Key issues. The fundamental questions that an organization must address in the strategic planning process in order to become more effective and successful.

Management. Facilitating decision making in an organization so that it can achieve its goals.

Mandate. The range of material culture for which the organization takes responsibility (such as types of media, disciplines, and geographic and chronological range) and the organization's reach in terms of audience (whether local, national, or international; focused on a particular age, on families, on seniors, and so on).

Master plan. Organization of functions and resources toward achieving a desired level of effectiveness, often reviewing all aspects of the institution and projecting requirements for additional space, staffing, or finances, as well as the means of attaining them.

Milestone. A significant point of achievement or development that describes progress toward a goal.

Mission statement. States the intent or purpose of an organization—its raison d'être.

Objectives. Short-term, quantified levels of achievement specified in plans and budgets as measures of longer-term, qualitative goals.

Operating budget. A projection of allocations for the institution's running costs, usually prepared annually.

Operating (or running) costs. Ongoing expenses of an institution, including costs for salaries and benefits, building occupancy, maintenance, security, administration, marketing, and public programming and education.

Organizational chart. A diagram of an institution's management and staff structure.

Outcomes. Desired changes in behavior—among visitors, stakeholders, donors, staff, volunteers, and community members—that result from achieving the goals for your institution.

Performance indicators. Statistics, ratios, costs, or other ways of measuring progress toward achieving the aims and objectives of the organization, such as cost per guest or revenue per guest; such indicators should be used with caution because they do not usually refer to the quality of the experience.

Policy. A statement of the organization's commitment to its mission, mandate, and purposes in relation to a particular function and to the achievement of specific levels of quality.

Public trust. Responsibility (in some jurisdictions, a legal responsibility) for the collective natural, artistic, scientific, or material heritage of others assumed by the governing body of the institution; the institution is entrusted to care for that heritage not only for members of the present generation but also for their descendants in perpetuity with the same prudence that one would be expected to exercise if the property were one's own.

Retreat. An extended workshop at which participants use brainstorming and open discussion to consider long-term plans, often as part of a strategic planning process.

Stakeholders. Those people who have an investment in the success or failure of the mission of an institution.

Statement of purpose. A concise identification of the functions of an organization in relation to the objectives defined in its mandate.

Strategic directions. Meaningful and memorable guidelines indicating an institution's approach or philosophy in resolving the key issues affecting it.

Strategic planning. The process of determining the optimal future for an organization and the changes required to achieve it.

SWOT analysis. An analysis of an institution's strengths, weaknesses, opportunities, and threats.

Task force. A group of individuals, usually from different departments, who cooperate to achieve a common aim, such as an exhibition.

Tasks. The particular steps that are needed to fulfill an objective.

Trust. *See* **Board**.

Trustee. A member of a board or trust in either a governing or advisory role.

Trustee's manual. A publication providing members of the organization's governing or advisory board with all relevant mission, mandate, and policy statements, as well as the board constitution, a history of the institution, current plans, staff organization charts, budgets and financial reports, board roles and responsibilities, and an outline of the committee structure.

Vision statement. Text that expresses the impact the institution would like to have.

Volunteer. An unpaid employee, whose rewards are in the form of personal development and social recognition for work done.

Work plan. A statement of objectives and resources, together with a budget and a schedule for achieving particular tasks.

Zero-base budgeting. A method of projecting revenue and expenditures that requires managers to justify each allocation in relation to the programs it makes possible without reference to historical levels of service provision.

Bibliography

Accredited Museum. *Accreditation Guide—Section One: Organizational Health.* Arts Council England, June 2014. Accessed July 25, 2016. www.artscouncil.org.uk/sites/default/files/download-file/FINAL_201406_GuidanceSection1_PrintFriendly.pdf.

Allison, Michael, and Jude Kaye. *Strategic Planning for Nonprofit Organizations: A Practical Guide and Workbook.* 3rd ed. Hoboken, NJ: John Wiley & Sons, 2015.

American Alliance of Museums. "Characteristics of Excellence." Accessed August 15, 2016. aam-us.org/resources/ethics-standards-and-best-practices/characteristics-of-excellence.

———. "Core Documents." Accessed August 15, 2016. aam-us.org/resources/assessment-programs/core-documents/documents.

———. *Organizing Your Museum: The Essentials.* Washington, DC: Rowman & Littlefield, 2001.

———. *Stand For Your Mission: The Power of Board Advocacy: A Discussion Guide for Museum Trustees.* Washington, DC: BoardSource, 2016.

American Public Gardens Association. "Public Garden Sustainability Index: Start Here." Accessed July 25, 2016. publicgardens.org/sustainability-index/start-here.

Andringa, Robert C., and Ted W. Engstrom. *Nonprofit Board Answer Book: Practical Guidelines for Board Members and Chief Executives.* 2nd ed. Washington, DC: BoardSource, 2001.

Association of College & Research Libraries. "Assessment in Action: Academic Libraries and Student Success." Accessed July 25, 2016. www.ala.org/acrl/AiA#cycle.

Association of Zoos & Aquariums. *The Accreditation Standards and Related Policies, 2016 Edition.* www.aza.org/assets/2332/aza-accreditation-standards.pdf.

Baldwin, Joan H., and Anne W. Ackerson. *The Importance of Mission in Guiding Museum Practice: Essays from the 2002 series 3x3: Workshops for Museum & Not-For-Profit Leaders.* New York: Museum Association of New York, 2003.

Brinckerhoff, Peter C. *Mission-Based Management: Leading Your Not-for-Profit into the 21st Century.* 3rd ed. San Francisco: Jossey-Bass, 2009.

———. *Nonprofit Stewardship: A Better Way to Lead Your Mission-Based Organization.* San Francisco: Jossey-Bass, 2004.

Bryson, John M. *Strategic Planning for Public and Nonprofit Organizations: A Guide to Strengthening and Sustaining Organizational Achievement.* 4th ed. San Francisco: Jossey-Bass, 2011.

Bryson, John M., and Franum K. Alston. *Creating Your Strategic Plan: A Workbook for Public and Nonprofit Organizations.* 3rd ed. San Francisco: Jossey-Bass, 2011.

———. *Implementing and Sustaining Your Strategic Plan: A Workbook for Public and Nonprofit Organizations.* San Francisco: Jossey-Bass, 2011.

Carver, John, and Miriam Carver. *Reinventing Your Board: A Step-by-Step Guide to Implementing Policy Governance.* Rev. ed. San Francisco: Jossey-Bass, 2006.

Dayton, Kenneth N. *Governance Is Governance.* Washington, DC: Independent Sector, 2001.

Decker, Juilee. *Fundraising and Strategic Planning: Innovative Approaches for Museums.* Lanham, MD: Rowman & Littlefield, 2015.

Dickman, Sharron. *The Marketing Mix: Promoting Museums, Galleries and Exhibitions.* Canberra: Museums Australia, 1995.

Doré, Michael. *Thinking Strategically within Non-Profits.* 2nd ed. Austin, TX: 1st World Library, 2003.

Duncan, Miranda. "Effective Meeting Facilitation: The Sine Qua Non of Planning." *Lessons Learned, a Planning Toolsite,* 2004. National Endowment for the Arts, 6 October 2005. arts.endow.gov/resources/Lessons/DUNCAN1.html.

Fischer, Daryl, and Lawrence Butler. *Strategic Thinking and Planning.* Washington, DC: Museum Trustee Association, 2004.

Grace, Kay Sprinkel. *The Nonprofit Board's Role in Setting and Advancing the Mission.* Washington, DC: BoardSource, 2003.

Holland, Thomas P., and Myra Blackmon. *Measuring Board Effectiveness.* Washington, DC: Boardsource, 2000.

Houchin, Susan, and Candace Widmer. *The Art of Trusteeship: The Nonprofit Board Member's Guide to Effective Governance.* San Francisco: Jossey-Bass, 2000.

Hudson, Mike. *Managing without Profit.* London: Penguin Books, 1995.

Hughes, Sandra R. *To Go Forward, Retreat! The Board Retreat Handbook.* Washington, DC: BoardSource, 1999.

Ingram, Richard T. *Ten Basic Responsibilities of Nonprofit Boards.* Washington, DC: BoardSource, 2003.

King, Brad, and Barry Lord. *The Manual of Museum Learning*. 2nd ed. Lanham, MD: Rowman & Littlefield, 2015.

Kocsis, Deborah L. *Driving Strategic Planning: A Nonprofit Executive's Guide*. Washington, DC: BoardSource, 2003.

Kopco, Mary A., et al. *The Business of Museums: A Behind-the-Scenes Look at Curatorship, Management Strategies, and Critical Components for Success*. Boston: Aspatore Books, 2004.

Kotler, Neil, and Philip Kotler. *Museum Marketing and Strategy: Designing Missions, Building Audiences, Generating Revenue and Resources*. 2nd ed. San Francisco: Jossey-Bass, 2008.

Leblanc, Richard, and James Gillies. *Inside the Boardroom: How Boards Really Work and the Coming Revolution in Corporate Governance*. Mississauga, Ontario: John Wiley & Sons, 2005.

Lord, Barry. *Art and Energy: How Culture Changes*. Washington, DC: Rowman & Littlefield, 2014.

Lord, Barry, and Gail Dexter Lord. *Artists, Patrons, and the Public: Why Culture Changes*. Lanham, MD: AltaMira, 2010.

Lord, Barry, Gail Dexter Lord, and Lindsay Martin. *Manual of Museum Planning: Sustainable Space, Facilities, and Operations*. 3rd ed. Lanham, MD: AltaMira, 2012.

Lord, Gail Dexter, and Ngaire Blankenberg. *Cities, Museums, and Soft Power*. Washington, DC: Rowman & Littlefield, 2015.

Lord, Gail Dexter, and Barry Lord. *The Manual of Museum Management*. 2nd ed. Lanham, MD: AltaMira, 2009.

McCarthy, Conol, ed. *Museum Practice*. Vol. 2 of *The International Handbooks of Museum Studies*. New York: Wiley-Blackwell, 2015.

Merritt, Elizabeth. "How to Forecast the Future of Museums." *Curator* 54, no. 1 (2011): 25–34. doi:10.1111/j.2151–6952.2010.00062.x.

———. *Museums and Society 2034: Trends and Potential Futures*. Washington, DC: Center for the Future of Museums, 2008. www.aam-us.org/docs/center-for-the-future-of-museums/museumssociety2034.pdf.

———, ed. *National Standards and Best Practices for U.S. Museums*. Washington, DC: Rowman & Littlefield, 2008.

Merritt, Elizabeth E., and Victoria Garvin, eds. *The Secrets of Institutional Planning*. AAM Professional Education Series. Washington, DC: Rowman & Littlefield, 2007.

Moran, Barbara B., Robert D. Stueart, and Claudia J. Morner. *Library and Information Center Management*. Santa Barbara, CA: Libraries Unlimited, 2013.

Nadler, D. A. "What's the Board's Role in Strategy Development? Engaging the Board in Corporate Strategy." *Strategy and Leadership* 32, no. 5 (2004): 25–33.

Nelson, Sandra S. *Strategic Planning for Results*. Rev ed. Chicago: American Library Association, 2008.

O'Connell, Brian. *The Board Member's Book: Making a Difference in Voluntary Organizations*. 3rd ed. New York: Foundation Center, 2003.

Ontario Ministry of Tourism and Sport. "Standard for Community Museums in Ontario." Last modified November 2, 2015. Accessed July 25, 2016. www.mtc.gov.on.ca/en/museums/museums_standards.shtml.

Perrone, Michela, and Janis Johnston. *Presenting Strategic Planning: Choosing the Right Method for Your Nonprofit Organization*. Washington, DC: BoardSource, 2005.

Poister, Theodore H. *Measuring Performance in Public and Nonprofit Organizations*. San Francisco: Jossey-Bass, 2003.

Pokras, Sandy. *Team Problem Solving: Reaching Decisions Systematically*. Menlo Park, CA: Crisp Publications, 1989.

Public Library Association. "It's All in the Planning: Getting Started on Strategic Plans and Development Plans." Accessed July 25, 2016. www.ala.org/pla/onlinelearning/webinars/ondemand/planning.

Rakow, Donald Andrew, and Sharon A. Lee. *Public Garden Management*. Hoboken, NJ: John Wiley & Sons, 2011.

Robinson, Maureen K. *Nonprofit Boards that Work: The End of One-Size-Fits-All Governance*. New York: Wiley, 2001.

Saul, Jason. *Benchmarking for Nonprofits: How to Measure, Manage, and Improve Performance*. St. Paul, MN: Fieldstone, 2004.

Scott, Carol A. *Museums and Public Value: Creating Sustainable Futures*. Farnham, UK: Ashgate, 2013.

Steiner, Sarah K. *Strategic Planning for Social Media in Libraries*. Chicago: ALA TechSource, 2012.

Stromberg, John R., et al. *10 Must Reads: Strategies: Making Change Happen*. Edinburgh, UK: MuseumsEtc, 2014.

Suchy, Sherene. *Leading with Passion: Change Management in the 21st-Century Museum*. Walnut Creek, CA: AltaMira, 2004.

Varbanova, Lidia. *Strategic Management in the Arts*. New York: Routledge, 2013.

Weil, Stephen. *Making Museums Matter*. Washington, DC: Smithsonian Books, 2002.

Weil, Stephen, and Peggy D. Rudd. *Perspectives on Outcome Based Evaluation for Libraries and Museums*. Washington, DC: Institute of Museum and Library Services, 2000.

Index

Note: Italic page numbers refer to figures and tables.

About the Authors and Case Study Contributors

Joy Bailey-Bryant is the managing director of the U.S. office of Lord Cultural Resources. A cultural planning specialist interested in people's stories, she works with public officials, institutional leaders, and developers to creatively plan urban sites and bring people (life!) to public institutions. Joy led public engagement for the Smithsonian's National Museum of African American History and Culture, reaching thousands of stakeholders; the Chicago Cultural Plan, which is widely hailed as having "democratized" culture for Chicagoans; and the Albany Civil Rights Institute in Georgia, unearthing untold stories of the southwest Georgia civil rights movement. She is a graduate of Florida A&M University and American University.

Tricia Baldwin, MusBac, MBA, was the managing director of Tafelmusik Baroque Orchestra and Chamber Choir from 2000 to 2014 and headed the renovations and venue diversification during her time there. She was awarded the Canada Council for the Arts John Hobday Award in Arts Management in 2012. Tricia is currently the director of the Isabel Bader Centre for the Performing Arts at Queen's University in Kingston, Ontario.

Veronica Y. Blandon is a senior management consultant and leads business development for Latin America at Lord Cultural Resources. Working with boards, institutional leaders, and staff in not-for-profit organizations, corporations, and governments throughout Canada, the United States, Latin America, and western Asia, she has overseen the successful completion of more than forty-five projects. After earning a bachelor of arts with honors in economics from the University of Toronto, Veronica attained a certificate in social impact analysis from the Schulich School of Business. She is a Certified Human Resources Leader (CHRL) and is currently working toward an executive master of human resources management at York University. In 2016, she was awarded Best in Cultural Management by Build Global Awards.

Kathleen Brown has worked for more than three decades with public and private organizations at home and internationally. In her long engagement with Lord Cultural Resources, beginning as managing director in 1992, Kathleen established their U.S. operations. In 2016, she was appointed chief operating officer of the company, responsible for the day-to-day management of its offices worldwide and the coordination of all its functions—including consulting, planning, human resources, business development, and marketing. Kathleen is an active contributor to the Lord Cultural Resources professional manual series.

Kelvin Browne is the executive director and chief executive officer of the Gardiner Museum in Toronto. Prior to this he held several positions at the Royal Ontario Museum (ROM), including managing director of the Institute of Contemporary Culture and vice president of marketing and major exhibitions. Kelvin is well-known as a magazine and newspaper design columnist and wrote the book *Bold Visions* about the architecture of the ROM. He holds a master of architecture degree from the University of Toronto.

Virginia Eichhorn has been a director of the Tom Thomson Art Gallery (TOM), Owen Sound, Ontario, since 2009. For her thirty years in the visual arts, Virginia was awarded the Ontario Crafts Council Award for Curatorial Excellence in 2009. Under her leadership, the TOM received an "A" rating from the Ontario Arts Council. In 2014, she initiated a groundbreaking multiyear partnership for the TOM with Roots Canada, a leading lifestyle brand of stores in North America. In 2015, Virginia was part of a three-person team that developed an extensive five-year business plan for the TOM as well as a case for expansion and incorporation.

Dov Goldstein is principal consultant at Lord Cultural Resources. With over twenty years of experience in urban and cultural planning, Dov has led large projects for such organizations as the Canadian Museum for Human Rights, the King Abdulaziz Center for World Culture in Saudi Arabia, and Mexico's Museum of Energy and Technology. Dov's work includes strategic, cultural, and master planning, as well as project management and client representation services for museums, libraries, multiuse cultural developments and cultural institutions, and municipalities and private sector companies.

Sarah Hill, BCom, MA, a senior consultant at Lord Cultural Resources, has worked with numerous cultural institutions, focusing particularly on heritage sites. Prior to joining Lord, Sarah worked in Scotland with the Heritage Lottery Fund, a national funding agency. Sarah conducts master planning, strategic and business planning, audience and program development, and grant application writing. She also serves on the Toronto and East York Community Preservation Panel and Architectural Conservancy Ontario.

Susan Kent is the principal of S. R. Kent, a consultancy that serves libraries and other nonprofit organizations. She was the director and chief executive of the branch libraries for the New York Public Library, the city librarian and director for the Los Angeles Public Library, and the director of the Minneapolis Public Library. She serves as chair of the advisory committee for the American Library Association's Center for the Future of Libraries. She has been recognized as Librarian of the Year by *Library Journal* and was awarded the Lippincott Award for "service to the profession" by the ALA.

Julia C. Levy has more than thirty years of experience in the nonprofit sector. She joined New York's Roundabout Theatre in February 1990 and now serves as its executive director. Julia has helped guide its growth from a small off-Broadway company operating one theater to a leading not-for-profit institution with five theaters in the Broadway district. She works closely with the board of directors and oversees fundraising, government relations, arts education programs, archives, and institutional public relations. In 2015, Julia was named to *Variety*'s New York Women of Impact. She is a frequent lecturer on arts management, sponsorship, governance, and fundraising.

Gail Dexter Lord is cofounder and copresident of Lord Cultural Resources. With Barry Lord, she is coeditor of *The Manual of Museum Planning* (1991, 1999, 2012) and coauthor of *The Manual of Museum Management* (1997 and 2009). She also coauthored, with Kate Markert, the first edition of the *Manual of Strategic Planning for Museums* (2007). Gail's most recent book is *Cities, Museums and Soft Power*, which she coauthored with Ngaire Blankenberg in 2015. Gail has collaborated with museums and cities to create new kinds of institutions such as the Museum of the African Diaspora in San Francisco, the Foundling Museum in London, and the Canadian Museum for Human Rights in Winnipeg. Gail is a member of the Order of Canada (2016) and Officier de l'Ordre des Arts et des Lettres de France (2014). In 2016 she was awarded an honorary doctor of letters by McMaster University.

Kate Markert is executive director of Hillwood Estate, Museum & Gardens in Washington, D.C., where, as the result of a strategic planning process, a special exhibition program and revitalized gardens spurred a 50 percent increase in attendance over five years and tripled the membership. She has been director of the Wadsworth Atheneum in Hartford, Connecticut, associate director of the Walters Art Museum, and deputy director and acting director of the Cleveland Museum of Art. She is on the visiting committee of Longwood Gardens and is a member of the Association of Art Museum Directors and of the Directors of Large Gardens. She has a master of arts in art history and a masters in business administration.

Lauren Anne Merkel is a senior consultant in the New York office of Lord Cultural Resources. Her expertise lies in strategic planning and arts management consulting. Lauren has led transformational projects for corporations, governments, and nonprofit organizations, both domestically and abroad. Prior to joining Lord, Lauren held managing positions at Roundabout Theatre Company and Lincoln Center Global, the consulting division of Lincoln Center for the Performing Arts. She holds a master of business administration from McGill University and a bachelor of arts in journalism from the University of Richmond. Lauren is on the advisory board of World Music Institute.

Paul Redman, executive director of Longwood Gardens, oversees all aspects of the 1,077-acre garden, including over eight hundred employees, seven hundred volunteers, and an $80 million budget. Under Paul's leadership, Longwood embarked on a groundbreaking strategic planning process that resulted in a unified direction and a visionary site master plan to guide Longwood for the next forty years. Through diversified programming, attendance has increased 79 percent and membership has increased more than 300 percent in eight years. Paul also instituted initiatives to enhance accessibility to Longwood's education programs via live, online distance learning, and he established the Longwood Gardens Fellows Program. He received his bachelor's and master's degrees in horticulture. In 2015, Paul received the Professional Award from the American Horticultural Society (AHS).

Amy Roth is the chief planning officer of the Whitney Museum of American Art, which relocated in May 2015 from its Madison Avenue home of nearly forty years to a new building designed by Renzo Piano in Manhattan's Meatpacking District. Prior to leading strategy and planning for the Whitney, she was its director of corporate partnerships for nearly a decade. She also has worked as a foundation and government relations manager and a financial analyst. She has been on the board of directors of the Madison Avenue Business Improvement District for ten years and is an alumna of Columbia Business School and Harvard College.

Ted Silberberg is a certified management consultant who has specialized in the museum, cultural, heritage, and tourism fields for over thirty-five years, the past twenty-eight with Lord Cultural Resources. Ted is the senior principal at Lord Cultural Resources responsible for market and financial planning and has worked on numerous projects across Canada, the United States, and the world. Among these are three separate projects with the Toronto Zoo, one of which was its 2015–2020 strategic plan.

Priya Sircar is a senior consultant at Lord Cultural Resources, where she specializes in cultural planning for communities and strategic planning for museums, parks, gardens, festivals, and other organizations. Priya has spoken at events around the United States and advises the Asian American Arts Alliance. She is a 2016–2017 EmcArts Arts Leaders as Cultural Innovators (ALACI) fellow. Prior to joining Lord, Priya helped build the global cancer survivorship movement at the Lance Armstrong Foundation, now LIVESTRONG. She holds an MA in arts administration from Columbia University and a BA from the Plan II Honors Program at the University of Texas.

Juan Ignacio Vidarte is director general of the Guggenheim Museum Bilbao, Spain. He graduated with a degree in economics and business administration from the University of Deusto in Bilbao in 1978 and took postgraduate studies at the Massachusetts Institute of Technology in Cambridge, Massachusetts. In 1992 he became director of the Consortium for the Guggenheim Bilbao Project, where he managed construction and installation of the museum. In 1996, the board of trustees of the Guggenheim Museum Bilbao Foundation appointed him director general of the museum, a position he has held since October 2008 along with his responsibilities as chief officer for Global Strategies of the Solomon R. Guggenheim Foundation.

Lightning Source UK Ltd.
Milton Keynes UK
UKHW051311061022
410039UK00004B/242